10.95

# Toymaking with Children

Freya Jaffke

# Toymaking with Children

Floris Books

Translated by Susan Howard
Illustrated by Christiane Lesch

First published in German under the title
*Spielzeug von Eltern selbstgemacht*
by Verlag Freies Geistesleben, Stuttgart
Translated from the fifteenth German edition, 1987
First published in English by Floris Books in 1988
Reprinted in 1990

British Library CIP Data

Jaffke, Freya
Toymaking with Children
1. Toys. Making-Manuals
I. Title    II. Spielzeug von eltern
selbstgemacht. *English*
745'592

ISBN 0-86315-069-1

Printed in Great Britain
by Dotesios Printers, Trowbridge

# Foreword

This book of toys is a completely revised and expanded version of the original workbook, which appeared in English as *Making Soft Toys,* in 1981. Several new sections have been added, for example, on the meaning of play, in order to remind parents and others who wish to present toys to small children of their great responsibility. The description of the simplest toys and the manner in which children are stimulated by these toys to a wide range of play possibilities is intended to help adults to select appropriate toys for individual children, as well as actually to make the toys themselves.

I have frequently experienced the following: when a father or mother creates toys in the presence of children, quite new relationships to the toys as well as to their "producer" are found, and such an experience is another bit of life experience won by the growing human being. It is a great joy to facilitate the creative play of children and to arouse in exchange unconscious but deeply experienced gratitude.

With these ideas in mind I hope this little book will find its way into the homes of many parents.

Freya Jaffke
Spring 1985

# Contents

# The Nature of Play

## The Meaning of Play

What is play? What constitutes a toy? These are challenging questions. It is all too easy to confuse mere "busy-ness" with play. It is tempting to be satisfied when children are occupied with anything at all, and one rarely stops to ask what is at work in the child. However, with a few thoughts and examples we hope to encourage the reader to experience the joy of making his or her own observations and of achieving deeper insight into the nature of play.

Whenever we encounter children really playing we see that they are re-playing scenes from daily life. The adult is for them of the greatest significance. They look up to him or her. Children experience through adults how they conduct their lives: at home, on the street, in shops, in their dealings with others; how they care for family and household; how they control and use technology. All these experiences prompt the child to activity; we call this play.

Children derive the greatest pleasure from involved play processes requiring great effort. If, for example, five or six-year-old boys want to create a particular type of vehicle that they can climb into, such as an ambulance, they need not only creative imagination but also skill, patience and willpower. With the simplest materials, they go to work. A table, playstands (page 25), chairs, stools, and perhaps even smoothly planed boards are placed together or on top of each other. Everything is then covered over and hung with cloths. Clothespins are helpful for attaching things. Bark logs become fenders, headlights, exhaust pipe, gear shift and foot brake; a log slice becomes the steering wheel; a piece of bark, artfully placed, becomes the rear-view mirror. Woolen cords (page 32) tied together become a safety belt, woolen bands (page 31) become back-up and brake lights. The flashing light on the roof is operated by a child sitting atop the roof and turning his hand around.

Usually such play begins with only the idea of the particular vehicle and the desire to build it. It is during construction, as children work with various materials and with their playmates, that specific ideas arise for arrangement, equipment, and improvements, and each time

9

an idea takes on form, it is a source of deep satisfaction, as when, for example, the children have created a "real" rear-view mirror. Here we encounter a significant question: what is it that makes this piece of bark a rear-view mirror? The fantasy-world of childhood itself. Only so long as the imagination of these particular children wants to have it so, does the bark remain a rear-view mirror. A similar piece of bark might simultaneously serve a second group of children as a telephone receiver, an ice skate or a little boat.

Unwitting observers might ask themselves when the children will actually begin to play, as they always spend so much time "manufacturing" their play-things. With surprise they observe that after a very short time of actual use or even shortly before the completion, everything is dismantled, transformed, or built up somewhere else. But playing means to be involved in process, not merely using or "operating" a finished product.

Human beings in general, and small children in particular, are beings in the process of becoming. In his surroundings the child needs that which is in the process of becoming, and needs the possibility to transform and to create anew. It is not the finished, completed object which is refreshing, satisfying, and invigorating for children. This is particularly true for individual toys. A toy actually needs only to express a characteristic quality, so that each time the child looks at it, the child's imagination is reminded of something different out of the child's growing life experience. A crooked branch with many little side branches and twigs, completely covered with a cloth, can be a mountain in a landscape; half-covered it can be a dwarf's cave, a dollhouse, or a barn. A little boy once held such a branch above his head and strode regally through the room as a great stag. Another child took the branch first as a scythe and cut the grass, then as a wind instrument as he sat with it among other child "musicians". A split log with a small protruding branch became a locomotive, a gasoline pump, a radio, an iron, and last of all a slide on the doll's playground.

Not every toy can be transformed on this scale and of course we also give children things which are more formed and where a typically human or animal figure, a bridge, or a wagon is recognizable. These toys, however, do not need to constitute the majority of playthings in a child's room. Those materials which support and encourage the kind of play indicated above will best nourish the imaginative strength of the young child which develops into the faculties and capacities needed during the school-age years and later in life. In such play the child can experiment freely and become acquainted with the world by being active. In a profound manner the child unites himself with the world creating self-confidence and a sense of security.

Most adults find it difficult to think their way into the child's imaginative world and its workings. All too easily adults seek to share with children their own joy, pleasure and sense of enchantment in looking at miniatures, perfect imitations, or even distorted caricatures of human beings and animals. However, "such pleasures give the children no experience of paradise; on the contrary, they serve to trivialize it for them. Play, activity rather than pleasures, keeps children happy. A toy gives a certain pleasure through its appearance; true delight arises only from using it. That which brings happiness and bliss and which endures, is simply activity itself; the games of children are nothing more than the expression of serious activity in the lightest winged cloak." (Jean Paul, in *Levana*.)

# Play: a serious activity

The play of the child is never superficial; it is a deeply serious activity. If this is not the case it is most often either the attitude of the adults or the quality of the available toys which causes children to lose their innate ability for absorbed play. Some basic pedagogical insights can help us here.

One should never forget that one's actions and the manner in which one acts, may have a profound effect on children. The child absorbs any experience of adult activity in his surroundings, and acts it out in imitation, this being the essence of free play. It is important to be aware that different sorts of adult activity, either very physically engaging such as washing the car or more passive such as reading the newspaper, will affect the child in a more or less stimulating way.

The fact that the child learns through imitation means that adults should behave in the presence of the child in a manner worthy of imitation. One can become so strongly aware of this that one eventually can become capable of leading the young child much more through imitation than through explanations and commands, which appeal to the child's reasoning ability, which is still only gradually developing. Adults can slip much too easily into the desire to instruct, which corresponds to their own advanced state of consciousness and is therefore easier for them than being a model for imitation, which demands much more self-discipline.

# The connection between play and work

Viewed from the adult perspective, play and work appear to be opposites, but on closer observation they can be seen to be directly related aspects of human activity.

The manner in which a child plays often reveals the way he will develop later in life. Rudolf Steiner observed, "A child who is slow in his play will be slow also in his thinking, in everything which is usually summed up as life experience."* Elsewhere he said, "He who has

* Conferences, June 14, 1920.

an eye for such things can foresee from the tendencies developed by a child in his play much about his future psyche, character, an so on. The capabilities of a human being in one area or another can be foreseen from the way in which the child plays."*

The same seriousness with which the child plays will later reappear in his work as an adult. One difference between child's play and adult work is that work must adapt itself to the necessities of the outer world, whereas the play of the child arises from within, from the child's fantasy, without having to be justified as meaningful behavior toward others or toward the activity itself. Such inner life is always accompanied by joy and pleasure and when acted upon give rise to a deep feeling of satisfaction. Although children may not be able to express these feelings in words, it will be apparent through their harmonious behavior, their eagerness, and often also in their glowing cheeks and shining eyes.

It is mistaken to think that the main purpose of play is to expend energy. Wild behavior is inappropriate for the human being and not a justifiable form of play for the child. Wildly romping children become overexcited and out of control; they no longer heed the words of an adult and are unable to quiet themselves or find a more peaceful game without adult help. Play at its best arises from a balance between inner creative

impulses and external circumstances. The child's essential, purposeful movement should never be confused with wild romping and horseplay.

Through closer observation of three clearly delineated stages of play, we can see how differently children of different ages behave in their play.

* Soul Economy and Waldorf Education, December 1921, Lecture 7

# Stages of Play

## Birth to the third year

In this first period children take possession of their own bodies. In this process, habit, imitation and constant unconscious repetition play leading roles. Tirelessly the child strives for the upright stance and is not discouraged by any failure. Without external pressure, simply by imitating the adults around them, children pursue their goals of uprightness and mobility, and thereby experience a quite new relationship to the three dimensions of space. In the same way children acquire speech and with it the foundations of thinking. Having in this way gained mastery over their bodies, children now begin to accompany their parents in their household occupations. In so doing, they reach a new stage of imitative learning. Choices become increasingly individual, less and less generalized, so that personal relationships with certain adults acquire significance in terms of the child's destiny.

The adult's actions are absorbed not consciously but lovingly. At first, children limit themselves to apparently purposeless imitative activity. They go around the room like their mother, picking up things which she has just tidied away, only to put them down again somewhere else. When the mother fills her basket with potatoes, the child fills a basket or cart with building blocks. Filling it once is not enough, however; otherwise the child would not empty it again and again with great zeal. The child does not understand as yet the purpose of actions, this is clear from the way in which, when allowed to be occupied with dustpan and brush, he or she will sweep in corners and from under the cupboard just like an adult, but never manage to sweep up the smallest bit of dirt!

Whether playing alone or with brothers and sisters, the child's favorite activity is repeatedly to build a tower of blocks higher and higher until it topples. In the sandbox children fill and empty their pails, letting the sand run over their legs or through their fingers with obvious enjoyment. They amuse themselves similarly with a basin of water. If, at the age of two or three, the child takes part with older siblings in playing "house", one can see that the little child does not grasp the actual point of the game until a later phase, in which the actions of adults are turned into a "let's pretend" game. Thus a little child may actually eat the grass intended to be salad or the sand intended to be the pudding.

These few examples demonstrate how the child unites effort, earnestness and eagerness with activity, which of course also includes enthusiasm, joy and delight, and each new step of development is achieved through imitation. I have noticed that children who have not been allowed to learn through imitation but have been brought up through constant appeals to reason and commands to make them behave in a certain way, even in their fourth year, tend to be pale, show little initiative, and have difficulties making contact with playmates.

# The third to the fifth year

During the second period from about the third to the fifth year (one could call it the age of imagination) quite new faculties develop. All the intensity which went into learning to stand, to walk, to speak, and to begin to think now finds a new field of endeavor.

A four-year-old watches her mother preparing a meal. She fetches an empty basket for a pan, covers the bottom with chestnuts and acorns for potatoes and begins to "cook". A little while later she collects the acorns and nuts together in a cloth and decorates the parcel with flowers and ribbons. She presents it with great solemnity to her mother because, "It's your birthday." A moment later she has unfolded the cloth and spread it over the top of the basket, which is now a bath tub. She bathes her doll, using an

acorn as soap. Then the cloth becomes a towel, the acorn a baby's bottle.

Another child finds a long thin bit of wood. It seems to him to be suitable for an iron, so he arranges a stool for an ironing board and play-cloths for laundry. Soon the iron and board together with another short branch have become a steamroller, the freshly ironed clothes are now a road. A little while later the overturned steamroller has become a ship with a helmsman and a captain.

These examples are enough to show what is characteristic for this age. The most remarkable feature is the child's ability to create "real" things out of simple objects in the environment (a log-iron, acorn-potatoes). The child's actions are imitations of daily events, constantly changing with each new discovery. This is not unconcentrated play. It is the outward manifestation of the child's creative imagination.

# The fifth to the seventh year

The third stage can be recognized by the fact that the stimulus to action no longer comes exclusively from without, from the world of concrete objects, as described for the previous phase, but arises more and more within the child. Play is still oriented toward the active adults in the environment, but before the child begins to play there arises within a picture, a mental image of what he or she wants to do. For example:

Four five and six-year-old children are playing mothers and fathers. They discuss exactly who will play each role. When the "mother" wants to set the table, she finds only wooden plates available and sees that cups, saucers, coffee pot and milk jug are missing. She finds what she needs in a basket full of short lengths and disks cut from branches. During the "meal" a new project arises: the dwelling is to be transformed into a physician's office. Obviously, the children have a clear memory-picture of what is needed. When the furniture has been moved to create a waiting room and doctor's office, the details are worked out. For example, syringes, stethoscopes, bandages and medicine bottles are made in the simplest way out of sticks, cloths and cords. Carefully, the patients are put to bed, and other patients in the waiting room are consoled with magazines made of folded cloth.

Another group of five and six-year-olds is using small logs, bark, pine cones, pebbles, and simple carved wooden figures of people and animals to build a farm on the floor complete with farmhouse, stables, a well, pastures and fields. The rooms are comfortably arranged, the animals cared for, the shepherd is led out to pasture with his sheep. For several days the children may continue to expand this scene. They add something here, change something there, obviously because the original design no longer corresponds to the constantly changing pictures arising in their imaginations.

The overflowing fantasy-world of the second period of play is more strongly colored now with visual imagery, and leads to ever more purposeful action. For example, children now enjoy making up little stories which they enact themselves (dressed up in pieces of cloth), or use dolls to enact play for the entertainment of the other children. Their powers of imagination are clearly revealed when they model with beeswax or clay, do simple handwork, or paint with watercolors or crayons.

Summing up the three stages, we can say that during the first seven years children are coming to grips with their world in ever new ways through active creative play. This constant activity engages them in a wealth of sensations, sense-impressions, connections, and finally also images, experiences and insights. It is a universal learning process, which reveals itself step by step to the careful observer. It is important that children be allowed to pass through each stage in the way described, and not be hindered in their development by intellectual content or abstractions introduced too early.

# How can we Help Children Play?

It is clear that not all children can play with a sense of fulfillment. More and more children need appropriate guidance. If one is aware of the particular developmental stage of the child and is oneself inwardly active and creative one will soon find ways to lead a child into play.

In the first phase, up to the age of two and a half or three years, if development is healthy, problems usually arise only if the adult surrounds the child with admonitions: "No, don't do that. Get away from there," and so on. A child who has just taken her first steps conquers her immediate environment through touching, patting, pounding. She pulls toward her everything that is not nailed down. The fact that her full attention is drawn to every new impression can be used pedagogically by distracting her to something she is allowed to do. This requires constant forethought on the part of the adult, which, though demanding, will assist a healthy unfolding of the will. A regular daily rhythm with a balance of waking and sleeping time is always essential.

In the second phase, from about the third to the fifth year, the most everyday events provide helpful stimuli for the child's play, if the adult takes them up in a simple way and enlivens them. There is so much to tell about the mailman, the farmer, the waiter in a restaurant, the doctor or the nurse; not thrust upon the child, but simply told with enthusiasm as one carries on one's work.

When possible allow the child to take part in real work. Sooner or later some activity will appeal and the child will initiate his or her own play. It can also be a help to include the "doll children" in one's daily activity and bestow upon them the same care one gives one's own children. After a while only a small reminder will be necessary and the children will take on their care themselves. The adult, however, should stay in contact with the nature of this kind of play.

Another stimulus for creative play can arise when the adult speaks of the "needs" of the playthings; for example, the train would like to take a long trip and the passengers who want to go along for the journey are already waiting; a doll is having a birthday and presents need to be wrapped, a birthday cake must be baked and the birthday table set; the boats need a lake with stones and shells and a boat house.

In the third stage, between five and seven years, the approach described previously can be continued and expanded. For example, near one's workspace in the kitchen, a "restaurant" can be added on. The waiter enjoys taking the orders and serving the most delicious dishes. Or by using cooking spoons and a string, one makes a telephone line to the "doctor." He answers his calls, bandages a wounded foot and prescribes a list of "remedies." In such play, the adult does play along without, however, leaving his own work except for brief moments. Thus the child has the active, purposeful adult in his presence and can imitate as much from him or her as is appropriate to his age level. The adult's imagination, even when quite contained, can give wings to the child's own emerging or developing joy in play. Being an adult caring for children can be experienced as the most difficult and at the same time the most rewarding of all professions.

# How does the Environment Affect Children?

During the first six or seven years the child is totally open to all experiences in his or her surroundings. All impressions are absorbed deeply, and, it could be suggested, influence the organic functions and structures which are still establishing themselves during this time. This would mean that the formation of the organs is inwardly completed under the imprinting influence of outer experiences. The child absorbs everything in his environment without a sophisticated capacity for distinguishing good from bad, helpful from harmful.

So that growth can occur in the most efficient and unhindered way possible, conscious care is required regarding the colors, the sounds, the playthings, and the human surroundings of the child. The idea that a modern child should adapt immediately to everything ignores completely the laws of development.

Subtle solid colors without "juvenile" patterns on the walls and in the fabrics of the child's room allow the eye to dwell on them in peace and to absorb the true qualities of the colors. When the simple melodic line of an adult voice speaking or singing, or the gentle sound of a

17

stringed instrument such as the lyre, is compared with noises produced by technical means (radio, TV, and so on) we gain some insight into the means by which a subtle, differentiated capacity for listening or singing can be nurtured or spoiled.

In the same way the greatest value must be placed on the quality of the materials of toys. In sympathy with the developing formation of the organs of the child, play materials from the organic realm would seem to be particularly appropriate. The variety of their forms, the quality of their surfaces, their natural density and weight are unmatched experiences. Natural materials greatly extend the range of experience of the child and enhance his or her sensitivity. Even the simplest objects provide the child with food for the imagination, as has been shown in the examples given earlier.

In addition to the things which we find ready made in nature as "toys", we can add those objects which have been formed by the human hand through craft work. Bearing in mind the significance of the unfolding of imagination, one should make such toys as simple and beautiful as possible.

# Which Toys for which Ages?

The descriptions of play already given have shown how simple playthings can be and yet what high standards should be set for the quality of materials. Those simple playthings which have been mentioned are precisely those which are most difficult to acquire, because they are not to be found in toy stores. Thus we are challenged to acquire a special eye for suitable things to be found on our walks or on excursions. With a little effort, one can also find stores which carry solid-color natural fabrics and yarns.

## One to three years

Since children at this age spend much time in the presence of a caring adult and love to play with pots and pans, cooking spoons, and so on, a very few things in the child's play corner are sufficient:
— large knotted dolls, about 28" (70 cm) square fabric, head approximately 5" (12 cm) diameter. (See page 54)
— simple doll-carriage, preferably wicker
— basket of building logs
— basket of chestnuts (conkers)

— carved scoop or shovel
— carved wooden human figures
— rocking horse.

Animal toys can easily be left to the next age group.

# Three to four years

All those things mentioned in this book in the sections, "Building on a Large Scale" (page 25), "Building on the Floor or on Tables" (page 35), and "The Play Store" (page 71). In addition:
— knotted dolls (page 54)
— soft doll bed
— various baskets and wooden bowls
— shepherd and sheep
— wooden horse and wagon or carriage
— wooden top.

So-called movable toys, such as two hammering or sawing figures on a push-pull bar; or, on a circular board, pecking chickens which are tied with strings to a movable ball below.

# Five to seven years

A few things may be added to the preceding list.
— knot dolls (if desired by the child, legs may be made from the two remaining corners of the fabric)
— flopsy doll (page 62)
— formed doll (toward the seventh year)
— doll clothes
— simple marionettes
— knitted animals
— a few good picture books, for special moments

— a handwork basket with the child's own scissors, needle book, thimble, spools of thread and bits of beautiful fabric and felt.

One should also note that the kinds of playthings mentioned in this book will also grow along with the child; that is, the child will find a new relationship to them at each new stage. In the fifth year, the joy of discovery awakens. For example, from an idea and a bit of effort a small round piece of wood with a string attached becomes a "telephone receiver." Perfect reproductions of objects from the adult world actually limit this joy of discovery and impede the emerging imagination. (See "The Meaning of Play", page 9.) Likewise technical toys such as remote-controlled cars, and electric trains should be reserved for a later age.

It is not always easy at home to maintain such a selection of playthings without compromise. One can overcome the difficulties in dealing with generous, well-meaning relatives by making one's wishes known well in advance. It is possible that if one makes the effort to share one's understanding of the development of the child, while joyfully anticipating things which may be created out of a desired material (for instance, silk cloths for marionettes), and describing the child's play with the new toys, one will be well rewarded. The insights which then arise in the gift-givers will help them to respect the parent's attempts at a certain strictness and consistency.

# The Doll: One of the Most Important Toys

When selecting toys, the most important consideration is that they should stimulate the child's imagination and provide images of a living, natural kind (hence, sections of branches rather than mathematically structured building blocks). These considerations apply especially to dolls. A doll is an image of a human being and is therefore the toy most suited to develop and enliven the self-image in the growing child. This has two consequences. Firstly, it would be a mistake to prevent small boys from playing with dolls and to restrict such play to girls, under the erroneous impression that it is a "motherly activity." Such discrimination between the sexes is pedagogically meaningless and ignores what is actually important for this age. Secondly, from this point of view, it would be the worst possible thing to give the child a doll complete in all anatomical details, technically so perfect that it can open and close its eyes, can be fed, can wet its diapers, and so forth.

The child would then have little use for the power of imagination. This power needs to be used, however, and often atrophies only because it finds insufficient opportunity to be used and strengthened. Just as human muscles are strengthened by regular use, so does the child's imagination need to be used in order to grow. In view of the manufacturers' efforts to produce ever more detailed dolls, it is not surprising that children appear to become increasingly demanding. The novelty soon wears off, however; the tricks needed to activate the technical arrangements, such as "speaking," soon become boring. The permanent frozen smile on the masklike features, the grotesque position of the fingers of the average so-called beautiful doll, need hardly be mentioned.

The simple knotted doll cannot be bettered, for children bring to it the inexhaustible profusion of their own imaginings. Indeed, it is only through fantasy that the knotted doll becomes a doll at all, and thus a living image of the human being. Such a simple doll enables the child through the power of imagination to embody every possible view of the human being in a perpetually changing, mobile, living way.

Today there are many children whose imagination is so stunted that they do not know what to do with a simple knot doll and must rely on an adult's suggestions. It is often surprising how rapidly this loss of a child's natural gift can be made good if the necessary means are given to the child. However, after the age of five this is only possible to a limited degree. If the parents can find a relationship to the knotted doll, then the child can imitate this. If this is not possible, and there are many understandable reasons for this, it would be preferable for the parent to make a plain stuffed rag doll with simple little clothes than to buy a manufactured doll from the toy store.

# Outdoor Play

For outdoor play, the most important item is the sandbox. It should not be too small or too shallow. Sand is an ideal play material for a child's hands, which constantly want to form and transform. Sand play can be enriched by adding sturdy shells and interesting stones. Little buckets, small wicker baskets for sifting sand, wooden shovels, and logs or branches in various forms provide stimulation for a wide variety of creative play.

A play corner outside the sandbox is desirable, especially when it contains a long tree trunk, a variety of long thick logs, and several smooth boards. With these the children can construct tables, stools and benches for little houses, a seesaw, a steamroller, and much more,

21

according to their ages. In this situation children have the possibility for real play. A swing is of course particularly nice. However, one should avoid constructing playground equipment such as immovable train structures, climbing apparatus, slides, an so on. These cannot be transformed, which means that they are inappropriate for real play. They are not open to the child's need for transformation and inventiveness. Instead, the child can only learn — often to the adult's delight — to "operate" the equipment.

In addition to the sandbox and play area, it is ideal if one has access to a meadow with trees and bushes and, if possible, a hard surface of stone slabs. Here, too, tree trunks or limbs can provide ideas for creative play. Children can also jump rope, play ball, walk on stilts or play with spinning tops. Older children can draw hopscotch games with colored chalk. "Doll mothers" can spread out their domestic play under the shade of a tree or a large sun umbrella.

Beyond all of these play possibilities, it is of course important that children have opportunities in parks or on walks in the woods to run, to play catch, tag or hide-and-go-seek, or to roll wooden hoops.

# Play and Clean-up Time

Playing and cleaning up belong together like inhaling and exhaling, sleeping and waking. Thus it makes sense to plan a clean-up time at the end of playtime or for the whole family at the end of the day, in which adults and children too, as they grow older, bring order into the surroundings and return each object to its own habitual place. When this activity takes on significance in the same way as cooking, mealtimes, or going for a daily walk, then it will no longer be experienced as a burden, but simply taken for granted. Pleasure and satisfaction will arise and this ordered environment will accompany the children into sleep or lead them to other activities.

If toys are kept in baskets on shelves behind a curtain, then they can easily be found and put away again. A toy chest into which everything that is lying around is tossed and then covered over with a lid is not to be recommended. Such a toy chest does not help the child to develop a sense of order and care for the environment; it simply conceals disorder.

Problems with cleaning up often arise merely because too much is expected of children before the age of six. The child who is admonished, "You are big enough to clean up all by yourself," finds himself confronted by an overwhelming task. Working with others, however, tidying up itself becomes play. The child can transform the concept of "clean-up" into images of lively activity. "The train has to drive to the train station; the ship must sail into the harbor; the delivery man brings the chairs back to the table."

Up to the age of three, children will industriously join in the adult's activity, helping to collect playthings and fill up the baskets. One cannot, of course, expect that the playthings find their way to the correct baskets, but the adult can complete the task with care. The mere activity of collecting and carrying objects back and forth is all that the young child can perceive and imitate. Between the ages of three and six years, cleaning up is alive with possibilities for creative play. If, for example, it is a matter of putting building logs back into a large basket, then one can see how a four and a half-year-old boy constructs a kind of "dump truck" and lets one piece of wood after another slide over it into the basket. Or during the folding of play cloths suddenly the idea for an ironing machine occurs, and the cloths, after being folded once the long way, are slowly pulled across a low stool and then folded again until they are all done.

All of this shows us that cleaning up should not be hurried. On the other hand, one must always notice the point at which the clean-up activity becomes too playful. One should then reassert actual cleaning. Children between the ages of five and six can take over simple tidying up activities — straightening up the doll corner, sorting the nuts in the play store baskets, returning the baskets to their proper places, and so on. Once the children are of school age, more and more responsibility for clean-up activity can be entrusted to them. Nonetheless, they will remain dependent on the watchful eye and a helpful word from the adult. During creative play time one should as a rule try not to interrupt the children for clean-up activity. Some children are taught to clean up one set of playthings before taking out a new toy. However, this means a new beginning each time and interferes with a rich, constantly transforming creative play.

Parents and teachers who find pleasure in the activity of tidying up will discover that clean-up soon becomes a matter of course, especially if they do not make the activity appear unusual by lavishing praise on the participating child.

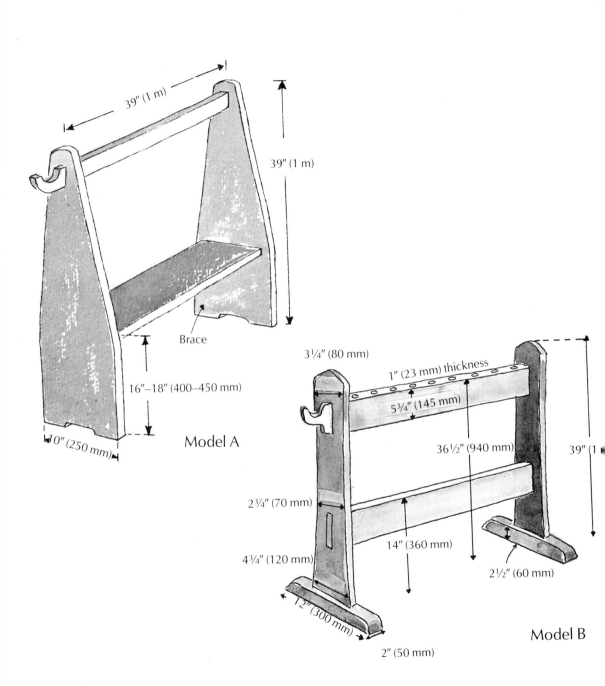

39" (1 m)

39" (1 m)

Brace

16"–18" (400–450 mm)

10" (250 mm)

Model A

3¼" (80 mm)

1" (23 mm) thickness

5¾" (145 mm)

36½" (940 mm)

39" (1

2¾" (70 mm)

14" (360 mm)

4¾" (120 mm)

2½" (60 mm)

12" (300 mm)

2" (50 mm)

Model B

# Forms of Play and Toys

## Building on a Large Scale

This type of building includes the making of houses, tents, boats, and vehicles by using tables, chairs, stools, benches, and so on. Children begin this kind of play between the ages of four and five (see also "The Meaning of Play", page 9). With this activity, children are following a primal impulse which can be observed in many children's games, namely creating a shelter into which they themselves can slip.

The most important materials with which we can provide children for this kind of activity are wooden playstands, building cloths, dress-up cloths (page 29), little sacks of sand (page 32), wooden clothespins, little wool rugs or old woolen blankets, crocheted crown headbands (page 31), cords (page 32), and wooden building logs (page 37).

## Wooden playstands

Wooden playstands are among those playthings which one would wish for every child's playroom. They can serve so many uses that they are nearly indispensable.

### Model A

Two such stands, with a cloth draped over them, can be a cozy doll corner or a little play store (page 71). With cloths pushed aside they provide the possibility for a tabletop puppet play (see standing dolls, page 45). A snug little bed is created by covering the board with a fleece rug and a play pillow (page 33) and hanging play cloths on both sides. (See playstand cloths, type B, page 26.) A doll's hammock (page 68) or a basket with crocheted cords (page 32) can be hung from the upper corners and the doll baby can be rocked or swung in its cradle. In any case, a brace should be constructed under the lower board so that the playstand is sufficiently sturdy.

### Model B

This playstand is easier for children to carry and is thus particularly suited for large-scale building. The upper cross-piece can be built so that it slides out; in that case it can be fastened on both sides with a removable wooden peg. One can hang hemmed play cloths like curtains from the playstands so that they will not slip off. Also small holes can be drilled in the upper cross-piece so that thin (³⁄₈", 10 mm) dowels can be placed across from one playstand to another to be used as an entrance or a roof. All edges should be rounded off. On the rounded hooks at the ends of the playstands (see illustration), ties can be hung for the "doors" (see playstand cloths) or a doorbell can be hung.

# Playstand cloths

*Material:* Solid-colored batiste (fine cotton) or other solid-colored lightweight cotton is best suited for playstand play cloths.

*Measurements:* Two lengths of 36" (90 cm) wide fabric, or one length of 45" (120 cm) or 60" (140 cm) fabric.

*Method:*
*Type A:* Cut length of each piece 45" (120 cm), finished length approximately 36" (90 cm), upper hem 4" (10 cm), lower hem 2" (5 cm).

*Type B:* Cut length 82" (210 cm), lower hems 2" (5 cm). Lay double and hem 4" (10 cm) in the middle for upper slide-through hem.

*Doors:* Cut length 40" (102 cm), finished length approximately 37" (95 cm), lower hem 2" (5 cm), upper hem about ³⁄₄" (2 cm). Sew into the upper hem a tie of the same fabric on each end: about 4" (10 cm) long and ³⁄₄" (2 cm) wide. The measurements for cloths for an entrance or for a roof vary according to the height of the arch. These cloths do not need to reach the floor, however.

Type A                          Door                          Type B

# Play cloths

## Building cloths

Solid-color cloths are among the most versatile materials that we can give children for their play. One can do almost anything with them. They can be used to build houses by hanging them from play-stands, tables, or chairs pushed together; they can be used as a landscape upon which to use building logs (as a meadow, lake, field); or as a sack to carry chestnuts, pine cones, and so on. Folded lengthwise they form the base for a homemade train (see trains from logs, page 43); folded in the same way and rolled up they become a fire hose. They are well-suited for all kinds of clothing and dress-up costumes. The child's imagination knows no limits and is challenged and stimulated by play cloths in a unique way. Little sacks of sand, like bean bags (page 32), are useful to weigh down and keep the play cloths from slipping off surfaces.

*Material:* Cotton muslin, gauze or poplin in various soft colors.

*Measurements:* For example, 36″ × 60″ (90 × 150 cm)

## Dress-up cloths

A lighter weight fabric such as cotton batiste (fine cotton) is particularly suited for dressing up, because it is easier to handle than the heavier muslin. These cloths may be used not only for dresses, capes, skirts, angel's wings, cloaks and head coverings of all kinds, but also as costumes for a particular character or role in creative play, such as doctor, nurse, fireman, mother, grandmother, king, princess, or bride. Crown headbands or wool cords can be used to fasten the cloths as belts or head-dresses (see page 32).

*Material:* Solid-color cotton batiste or very light muslin.

*Measurements:* For example 36″ × 48″ (90 × 120 cm)

30

# Crown headbands

These bands are particularly good for fastening dress-up cloths (see page 29) around the child's head and can also be used as belts or as swaddling clothes for dolls.

*Material:* Thick, soft sportweight wool yarn. Yellow yarn is particularly nice. Crochet hook.

*Method:*
1) Chain on 8–10" (20–25 cm) of loops (see arrow 1). Turn and single crochet back the entire length (arrow 2). For each stitch, poke the hook through the existing loop, hook the yarn and pull it back through the existing loop.

2) For the middle section, begin with 16" (40 cm) of chain stitches (arrow 3). Turn and make one chain stitch, a single crochet, half a double-crochet stitch (that is, loop the yarn once over the crochet hook, and then hook and pull the yarn through all the way) and then normal double-crochet stitches (arrow 4) until 2 stitches before the ★. Then again make half a double-crochet stitch, one single crochet, and a chain stitch.

3) Turn and make the other side accordingly (arrow 5): One single crochet, half a double-crochet stitch, then normal double-crochet stitches and at the end half a double-crochet and one chain stitch.

4) For the second tie, chain on 8–10" (20–25 cm) of loops (arrow 6), then turn and single-crochet the entire length. Make sure to secure the ends.

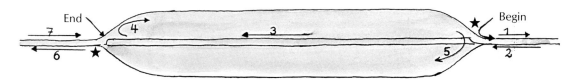

# Cords

One can hardly give children enough of these soft, thick woolen cords for their play. Children use them to tie and fasten their play cloths and dress-up cloths. Tied to a stick they become a fishing line; many tied together become a telephone line or the cable for a cabin lift. They can also be used to make a weighing-scale if the children have been lucky enough to see an old-fashioned scale. Sometimes they are also used very creatively to turn knot dolls (see page 54) into marionettes by tying them around the neck. With these few examples, perhaps the wide variety of uses for creative play can be indicated.

*Material:* Thick, soft sportweight wool yarn. Crochet hook, size J (Continental size 5 or 6).

*Method:* Using three to five strands of yarn together, chain 60 to 80 stitches, or any length desired. Finish off at both ends.

# Little sandbags

These can be used to hold building cloths in place on tables or other furniture, without the risk of scratches which can occur when using logs or stones. However, the child's imagination may also turn them into skis tied to their feet, weights for a block-and-tackle when tied to a cord, a fish at the end of a fishline, a stamp pad at the post office, or a load of lumber for a train, and so on.

*Materials:* Tightly woven fabric that will not allow the sand to trickle out; solid-colored cloth for a cover; approximately ¾ lb (350 g) of sand per sack.

*Measurements:*
7" × 5" (18 × 13 cm) finished size; for covers, cut fabric 5¾" × 19½" (14.5 × 49 cm)

*Method:* Cut the sack from the heavier fabric, fill with sand, and sew up completely. The cover can be sewn with no closure, so that it is easy to pull on and off for washing. First hem the short sides of the fabric, then turn inside out and fold the cloth into the size of the sand bag. Sew up seams on the long sides, finish off, turn and iron.

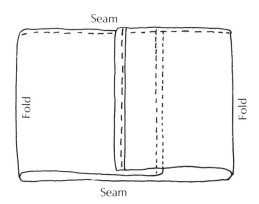

Seam

Fold

Fold

Seam

# Play pillows

Every child loves a soft pillow, filled with wool, that he can turn into a bed on the carpet or on a bench, sit on while playing on the floor, or tie with cords (see page 32) as a backpack or wear as a fire helmet.

*Measurements:* For example 12" × 16" (30 × 40 cm), finished size

*Material:* Simple muslin or remnants as a case for the wool batting; cover fabric (cotton corduroy is especially nice); cleaned, carded or combed sheep's wool.

*Method:* Sew up the case on three sides, stuff not too thinly with wool, then close the fourth side. Sew the case and cover the pillow.

# Building on the Floor or on Tables

Every child loves to take out all her playthings again and again and will use them all enthusiastically to build up the landscape for play. All this activity revolves each time around a human being; the child, as a ship's captain, needs a ship, and then a lake or ocean where shells can be found; as a shepherd, she needs a meadow with sheep and a house for the family; as a farmer, she needs a barn with animals, horse and wagon; as a railway conductor, she needs a train with passengers. The more the child is able to perceive the variety of the surrounding landscape directly or can experience it through stories, the more evident it becomes in the child's creative play: for example, a forest with homes for individual animals and a manger where they can feed; a mountain inhabited by many dwarves, with a cave where they can live.

Simple toys, carved or sewn, stimulate the child to surround them with a variety of things which are found readily in nature — roots, stones, shells, bark, pine cones, and fruits such as chestnuts and acorns. The essential element in all these things is that they are capable of making differentiated impressions on the developing sensitivity of the child. This is true for the subtle shadings of color, the forms, and the various qualities of materials such as stone, wood, wool, bark, and fabric.

It should be noted that children under the age of four are not yet able to create an imaginative landscape in a differentiated manner. At most they place many objects side by side in a small space and are finished as soon as the basket is empty.

# Building logs

Building logs of various lengths of branches with their bark left on offer a wide variety of natural forms and colors. Many, through their odd shapes, lend themselves to be seen as a variety of different objects from the child's daily experiences. Thus a curved branch can be a bridge, a sword, a trumpet, or a scythe. A protruding branch can become a water pump, the smoke-stack of a locomotive, the holder for a hanging doorbell or a part of a fence. In building a house, a lighthouse or another building, these logs are fastened together not mechanically by pushing a button or turning a screw, but through carefully balancing and manipulating the logs. The child thus develops an experience of the laws of physics.

*Materials:* Birch and other branches with nice bark, 1″ to 6″ (2 to 15 cm) in diameter.

*Method:* Saw the branches into lengths from 1″ to 10″ (2 to 25 cm). Larger limbs can be split with an axe. Slices can be sawn off the thickest limbs, roughly one or two inches (2.5 to 4 cm) thick. Leave side branches protruding a few inches. With a whittling knife or pocket knife, finish off the edges of the cut surfaces so that they are not too sharp. Sand the cut surfaces and apply beeswax or linseed oil, rubbing in well and polishing until smooth. Large wicker baskets are good for storing the logs.

The following are good playthings to go with the logs and are best stored in separate baskets: pine cones, pieces of bark, stones, shells, unspun wool, chestnuts, acorns, and feathers; also simple carved figures of people and animals (page 40), standing dolls (page 45) and dwarfs (page 48); small building cloths and clothespins.

# Small building cloths

Solid-colored fabric remnants in various sizes are a welcome enrichment for building on the floor (page 35). Often a small blue stream or lake is needed for a bark boat, or a brown covering for a branch to make a cave, or for a particular story a certain animal is needed that can be quickly formed by tying one or two knots in the fabric.

*Measurement:* 20″ × 20″ (50 × 50 cm)

# Pine cone birds

*Materials:* Pine cones, beechnut hulls, small feathers, pure beeswax of good quality, or glue.

*Method:* Fasten the head, made from a beechnut shell, to the pine cone body with glue or beeswax. With glue or beeswax fasten two or three feathers to the sides and tip of the cone for wings and tail feathers. A string can be tied around the body and fastened to a short stick so that the bird can fly.

# Bark boats

*Materials:* Pine bark pieces, small sticks, birch bark, feathers or fabric for sails.

*Method:* Bore a hole in the bark for the mast stick(s). Glue or nail the birch bark or fabric sails to the mast. Many variations can be made.

# Carved wooden figures

*Materials:* Birch branches, 1" to 2" (2 to 4 cm) in diameter; adjust length according to the width. Whittling knife or pocket knife.

*Method:* First round off the branch toward the top (in direction of arrow). Then cut in around the neck, making the head somewhat narrower as well. Make sure that the neck does not become a pointed groove. Facial features do not need to be indicated; however, by fastening a piece of a smaller branch at the back, hair braids or a bun can be suggested. One can also cut off the bark in such a way that it looks like a coat or jacket. Cut off the length of the body so that the head is a quarter of the total height of the figure. Rub the carved surfaces with beeswax.

# Carved wooden animals

By using crooked branches one can create toy animals which are very stimulating to the children's creative play. With a small saw, a sharp pocket knife, and a little imagination, one can discover many little creatures in branches lying on the ground or at the woodpile. All that is necessary is the appearance of a typical gesture or a characteristic trait; the child will complete the rest.

As an adult one may have a bit of difficulty at the beginning in learning to see gestures in the branches. However, if one simply collects a number of branches with joints and twigs that branch out, one will begin to discover more and more possibilities within them. Cover the carved surfaces with beeswax and rub in well.

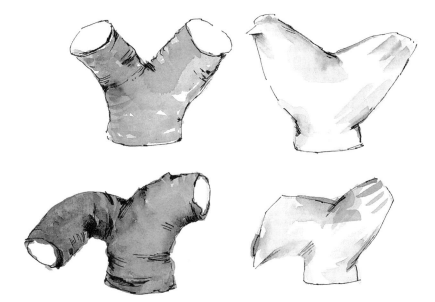

# Bridges

*Materials:* Branches which have formed appealing curves, wide or narrow, but not too thin: birch, chestnut, maple or nut trees, for example. Small camping hatchet, saw, whittling knife or pocket knife.

*Method:* With the hatchet, "carve" the upper surface. It is advisable to begin at the highest point and cut downwards on both sides until a nice, broad bridge surface has been created. It is easier to achieve if the hatchet is held close to its head and only small pieces are cut off each time. With a little practice one achieves accuracy and confidence in the use of the hatchet. The ends should be cut off at an angle so that the bridge has a stable base on which to stand securely. With a knife, smooth over the surface cut by the hatchet and round off the edges (this can also be done with a wood file or rasp). If desired, sand the carved surface smooth and apply beeswax.

# Trains made of bark-covered logs

Splendid trains in ever-new variations can be made when children are given a number of split logs, some with small protrusions, others somewhat carved out. Wheels are completely unnecessary if the children are given a narrow folded cloth as long as the train. The log with the small protrusion is usually the locomotive, and the little branch, covered with a bit of unspun wool, is declared the smoke-stack. Of course, the individual logs can be carved and should have a smooth surface on the bottom.

Play can be enriched by adding little uncarved twigs, a small bell, and passengers or freight from the child's usual assortment of playthings. If the child's playroom is carpeted, one must use smooth fabric such as satin or lining material underneath the train. Apply beeswax to all carved surfaces.

*Materials:* Various wooden branches covered with bark (birch, maple, chestnut or fruit trees), saw, hatchet, whittling knife or pocket knife, gouge.

# Cleaning and care of wooden toys

From time to time, wooden playthings rubbed with beeswax or linseed oil after they were carved can be easily and simply cleaned. The soil is only on the surface and can be easily removed.

*Materials:* 100% pure beeswax
— pure turpentine
— white rags (lint free)
— woolen cloth
— hot plate
— double boiler (or a can place inside a pan of water)

*Method:* Heat a small amount of beeswax in a double boiler (do not let it come to a boil). For 5 tablespoons of beeswax, only ½ teaspoon of turpentine is needed. Hold the soiled toy over the heat of the hot plate as well as the white rag which has been dipped into the beeswax mixture. The heat will melt the old wax on the surface of the wood and will loosen the dirt. If the toy is then rubbed with the warm washrag, the soil will be absorbed by the cloth and the wood will be newly waxed at the same time.

One must be very careful that the wax layer remains extremely thin; otherwise the wood will become sticky. If necessary, repeat the process a second time.

After the wood has cooled, polish with a clean wool cloth.

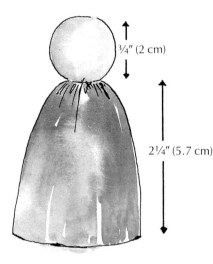

¾" (2 cm)

2¼" (5.7 cm)

# Standing dolls

Like the carved wooden figures (page 40), these standing dolls are particularly suited for children's building play on the floor or on the table. They can be made in various sizes and shaped to create an entire family. If kept very simple, they lend themselves to being transformed in creative play. For example, several shepherds in a hammock (page 68) might be seen from a boat as trout. Occasionally children will tie a small cloth around a figure for a particular character in a story.

*Materials:* Remnants of fabric or bits of felt, cotton knit (cotton jersey) for the head, white unspun sheep's wool for stuffing; yellow and brown unspun wool for hair; sewing kit.

*Method:* With a square of cotton knit, cover a bit of wool which has been plucked and rounded firmly into a ball; tie off at the neck. A head can also be made completely of unspun wool, in which case no eyes or mouth are necessary; form a cylinder of wool and simply tie off the head, taking care that it is nice and round. For the garment, a rectangular piece of fabric or felt (for a 2", 5 cm, head: 5½" × 9½", 14 × 22 cm, or for a 1¼", 3 cm, head: 3½" × 5½", 9 × 14 cm) is sewn together by joining the two longer sides to form a cylinder. The

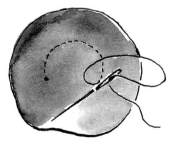

length of the garment is just barely three times the height of the head. Sew a running stitch along the upper edge and then attach the head to the body. A bit of colored unspun wool can be easily stitched to the head for hair or one can embroider hair with wool yarn. Eyes and mouth can be lightly suggested with a colored pencil. The garment can be stuffed with unspun wool so that the figure can stand more securely.

One can then clothe the figure with a shawl or cape. Hats can be made by sewing a running stitch around a circle of felt such that a wide brim is created. The running stitch is pulled together slightly and the hat is fastened to the head with a few stitches.

One should consciously avoid more detailed costumes and clothes such as aprons with ties, and so on, which are better suited to more formed dolls. Occasionally arms and hands are desired for standing dolls. These can be sewn using cotton knit and then tucked and sewn into the cloak.

# Gnomes

Children have a natural relationship to a variety of beings which surround us in different realms of nature. They hear about them in fairy tales, they accompany them in rhythmical movement, and they live with them in moments of deeply absorbed creative play in nature. They can also allow such beings to appear in the room, if the adults around them can develop a certain consciousness and love of truth regarding these realms. Often a few bits of colored unspun sheep's wool are sufficient to allow a dwarf or an elf to emerge. Sewn or even knitted gnomes require special care in a child's room. Their own special realm can be created, perhaps in a corner, among stones and roots and branches of all kinds.*

*Materials:* Bits of wool felt; unspun sheep's wool.

*Method:* Cut out the gnome's jacket (see illustration). Close the top seam of the hood and turn right side out. Sew a running stitch along the neckline, as indicated in the illustration by a dotted line. Stuff a bit of well-fluffed unspun wool into the cloak and hood, pull the running stitch somewhat together. Tie in the front

and fasten with a few stitches. Some of the unspun wool can be drawn out as a beard or sewn on afterwards. Wool can also be pulled out as hair around the face. Cut off surplus stuffing at the bottom, so that an even base is created for the gnome to stand. Such gnomes can be made in different sizes, with care to maintain the original proportions. Take care that the head is really large enough. These little gnomes can, of course, be carefully placed to stand together in a little basket, which can join the child's other playthings.

* See *Gnomes*, by Johanna Picht, Floris Books, 1989.

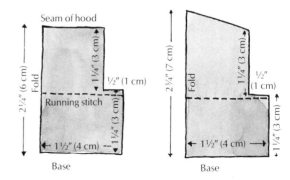

48

# Sheep from wool roving

These sheep are particularly good and easy to create in the presence of children. This also stimulates the children to make many sheep of their own. It is hardly necessary to give them help, for each little wool figure, even if it is just a simple tuft, already looks like a lamb.

When they have been use a lot they might need some repair. Simply loosen the neck-thread, undo the stitches holding the sheep together, wash the wool carefully, and after the wool has been slightly teased a new sheep can be created.

*Materials:* Wool roving, thread, a darning needle with a big hole.

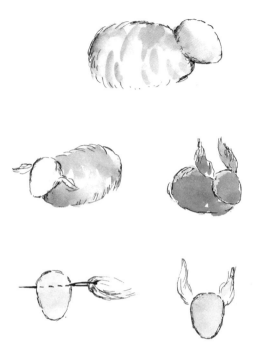

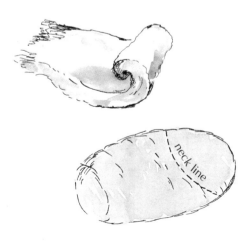

neck line

*Method:* Take a rectangular bit of wool roving, roll it up and sew it lightly together at the bottom. Tease a little wool out at either end to round off the ends and to make an egg-shape. Fasten with a few stitches. The same thread can be used for the neck. Stitch thread through at one end and tie off head (see illustration). Stitch through once more at the bottom and sew in. The neck thread has to be pulled tightly so that it becomes invisible.

For the ears, simply pull a bit of fleece with the darning needle through the head and round off the edges by shaping with your fingers. Rabbits and hares can be made similarly by folding the ears upwards.

# Pipe-cleaner sheep

This type of sheep is not really intended to be played with as a toy, and especially not by children under age six. Such sheep are especially nice in a Christmas creche scene. Adept children aged seven to nine can help to make them.

*Materials:* Long pipe cleaners or door-bell wire from the hardware store; wool roving in long continuous strands. Darning needle or carpet needle with very large eye.

*Method:*

1) For each sheep, take two equal lengths of wire or pipe cleaner, each 10" (25 cm) long, for example. The length of the wire determines the size of the sheep. One length forms the head and front legs, and the second length of wire forms the body and hind legs shape in the desired position. A sheep which is lying down does not need hind legs (see figure B); simply wrap the ends around the body section.

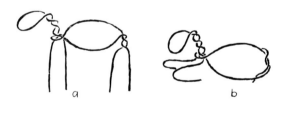

a

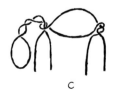

c

b

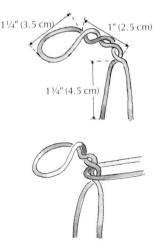

1¼" (3.5 cm)  1" (2.5 cm)

1¾" (4.5 cm)

2) Bend the first piece of wire in half. Twist the two ends together about 1½" (3.5 cm) down and form a noose for the head in an oval shape. Twist several times to form the neck, and spread the two remaining ends apart to form the front legs.

3) Bend the second piece of wire in half and loop it over the neck piece. Twist around once or twice tightly. The neck should not be loose or wobbly. After forming the oval body, twist the ends together one and a half times around and spread the rear legs. These measurements are only guidelines. A sense for the correct proportions will very quickly develop.

4) Begin the wrapping process with a long, thin strand of wool at the feet: the finer the strand, the better for creating a smooth wool surface. When all four legs have been wrapped, then wrap the head, the neck, and finally the body as thick as is desirable.

5) *Ears:* With the large-eyed needle, draw a strand of wool through the head. Pull over excess at ends and shape the ears somewhat (see illustration).

6) *Tail:* Pull out a very small bit of wool between two fingers held against the animal's rump. Twist and twirl the wool between your fingers so that the correct length and thickness is achieved.

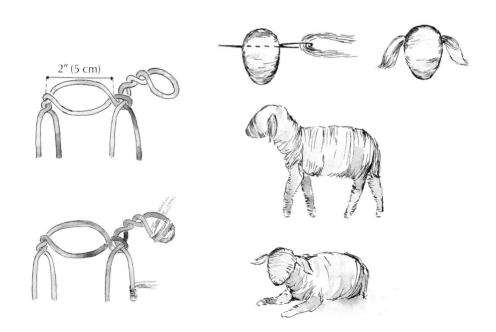

# Using unspun wool

## Teasing the wool

Cleaned, uncombed wool must be well-teased before it can be used for stuffing or for play. Teasing, however, does not mean tearing the wool apart! Simply take a small handful of wool — as much as separates easily from the rest — and using your two hands and your fingertips, carefully separate the fibers where they are most densely clumped together. The tuft should remain in one piece as it becomes much larger and more airy, like a delicate cloud or a veil. Repeating this process with tuft after tuft, a loose mountain of wool is created into which children love to plunge their hands.

Wool which has been teased in this manner can be readily formed into small human and animal characters. It is very elastic and smooth, without hard bumps when used to stuff or form a doll's head.

Allow yourself plenty of time for teasing wool. This activity radiates calm and involvement, and has a peaceful effect not only on the doer but also on the surrounding children. Depending on their age children will join in helping, shaping or playing with the wool.

If you use lots of wool often, then hand carders may be used. This activity is not nearly as gratifying for children as the teasing, although it achieves quicker results.

# The Doll Corner

With two playstands (page 25) or with one playstand and a shelf, a house corner can be created in which the children's dolls have their home. The playstands will be moved often by the children; the house will be rebuilt or additions will be made. Here daily life takes place through imitation. If we consciously do without real play objects such as a miniature stove, plastic pans, irons, and so forth, then we offer the child the opportunity to create or find "real" things again and again. In this manner a "bath-tub" can be created from an upside-down bench on one day and from a basket on the next. Two round slices of a log become the heating elements on the stove top or pot lids or waffle irons. A small piece of a branch becomes a cup, a hair dryer, an iron, and many other things as well.

Most important here, of course, are the dolls. When they are fashioned simply enough, they make possible the entire range of human appearance through the child's imagination (see also "The Doll: One of the Most Important Toys", page 20)

For the doll play, cloths for dressing (page 64), crown bands (page 31), yarn cords, and sheep's wool help children to create and dress doll children according to their age and experience. One can also give older children (five to six-year-olds) a simple doll's dress, perhaps with lovely simple embroidery (page 64). Bunting beds (page 66), various baskets, a cradle, a hammock (page 68), or a footstool can serve as sleeping places for doll children. Small wooden bowls and spoons, acorns and chestnuts, small vases and candlesticks, and a children's harp, greatly enhance the serious yet joyful quality of play in imitation of daily life or of special festive events.

# Knotted dolls and animals

*Materials:* Various solid-colored cloths and some unspun sheep's wool.

*Method:* For dolls, the head is formed by knotting one corner of the cloth, the arms by knotting two other corners. If the cloth is very soft and not too small, one

can pull out the cloth at the spot indicated in the illustration (✗) and make this into a simple knotted head. The two shorter ends can be knotted into arms. For a grandmother, one can add a kerchief from a bit of fabric. A grandfather or a shepherd may receive a bit of unspun wool tucked into the knot as a beard.

For animal figures, one can take the snail as an example. Tie a tiny knot at the very ends of two corners of the cloth. Then hold these two ends together and tie a larger knot as a head. With the remaining fabric, one can create the snail's shell, either by tying two more knots, one on top of the other, or by wrapping the cloth around one's hand and then tying the twisted fabric into a knot. According to the manner in which the knots are tied — either pulled and stretched, long or rounded, or with many knots of various sizes — the child's imagination has the opportunity to recognize familiar animal forms such as rabbits, foxes, sheep, and so on. One can also help to express the character of a particular animal through the color of the fabric which one selects. Thus a green knotted cloth could easily suggest a frog, whereas a blue one might be a bird in its nest.

# Simple unformed baby dolls

A mother, who chooses to give her child a simple unformed baby doll or knot doll because she senses that in so doing she can unfold certain forces in the child, should be aware that this also demands something very special from her as well, namely the love she bestows upon the doll which the child can then imitate. This love arises first through the care taken in the making of the doll and is sustained by consciously accompanying the doll inwardly as the child plays with it throughout the day.

*Materials:* pale rose-colored wool or flannel (silk for infants and young toddlers); unspun sheep's wool.

*Measurements:* 18″ × 24″ (45 × 50 cm) rectangle; 14″ × 16″ (35 × 40 cm) rectangle for the silk doll

*Method:*
1) Hem the edges of the fabric carefully by hand so that the hem is nice and soft.
2) Fluff the wool gently and thoroughly (see "using unspun wool", page 52), form it into a ball and cover it with fabric.
3) With a twisted strand of wool, tie off the head, making sure that it is not too tight and that all four corners hang down evenly.
4) Make a knot at the end of each of two

opposite corners for the hands, making sure that the arms are not too long.

5) Indicate eyes and a mouth very subtly with small colored pencil marks. It is advisable to give children several cloths for wrapping and dressing the doll (page 64).

With the silk doll, the wool can be pulled from the head down one and a half times the length of the head to form a body. This should also then be covered with silk stitched around it so that the child does not put the wool into his mouth. If the wool is carefully pulled from the head through the neck down into the body, this strengthens the head.

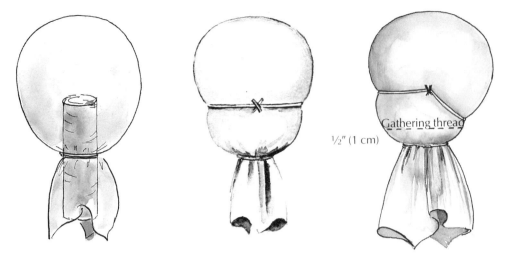

½" (1 cm)

Gathering thread

# Formed doll

The formed doll is for a later stage of development (see "The Doll: One of the Most Important Toys," page 20).

*Materials:* Light rose-colored or white cotton knit (perhaps from an old undershirt), unspun sheep's wool, strong white thread (darning thread, crochet thread or embroidery floss), wool or mohair yarn for hair.

*Method:* Measurements and directions are given here for a doll approximately 9" (22 cm) long. The doll can easily be made in a variety of sizes by using the head height as the unit of measurement for making the body. The proportion of head to body is roughly 1 to 3½. Therefore, make the head first, in any size you choose, and adjust the body measurements accordingly.

## The head

1) Fluff unspun sheep's wool and form into a ball which is firm and solid. Place the ball on a square of 8" × 8" (20 × 20 cm) cotton knit (cotton jersey or knitted cotton). Draw the fabric ends together and pull on them, holding tightly and adding more stuffing until a firm sphere is formed. Tie off at the neck. It is also very helpful to place a tightly rolled wool cylinder inside the neck before tying off the head; this will keep the neck from becoming wobbly later on.

2) Choose the smoothest aspect to be the face. Fasten a length of strong thread to the place where an ear would be, and bind it around the head horizontally once or twice, tightly enough to constrict and make an indentation at the eye line.

3) Stitch into the fabric at the starting point, then continue the thread halfway around the head to the other ear and stitch it down firmly.

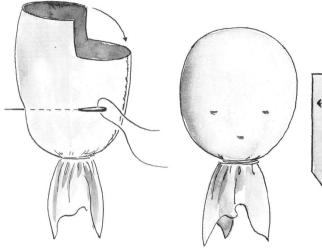
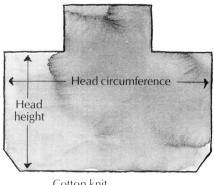

Cotton knit

4) Take the same thread over the top of the head and down to the opposite ear and pass it down through the neck in front of the cylinder, then stitch it down at the second ear, making sure not to pull it too tight.

5) To shape the back of the head, pull the horizontal thread down toward the nape of the neck to about ½″ (1.5 cm) above the neck thread. Smooth any bulges at neck upward under the thread. Do not cut off surplus fabric.

6) Cut out the outer covering for the head from cotton knit according to the illustration. The grain of the fabric should run vertically up and down the face, with maximum stretch horizontally. Allow 1″ (2.5 cm) above the head and 1½″ (3.5 cm) below

7) Smooth the fabric across the face, especially at the eye line. Overlap at the back of the head, turn under the raw edge and sew a vertical seam. Make sure

that the fabric is drawn tight. The seam can be quite wide at the neck to make sure there are no wrinkles in front at the chin.

8) Draw the top flap toward the back of the head, trim off excess fabric, turn under raw edges and sew together with small, tight stitches. The outer covering should fit tightly and neatly.

9) Use glass-headed pins to find the right place for the eyes. Then stitch in from the ear to the first eye, making one stitch just to right or left of the pin, and from there stitch through to the second eye, and then to the second ear. Pull thread taut. The eye stitch should be barely ⅕″ (5 mm) wide. Make sure that it is horizontal and that the distance between the eyes is not too small. 10) One can then cover the eye stitch with a blue colored pencil mark and indicate the mouth with a red colored pencil. Dots for eyes and mouth should form an equilateral triangle.

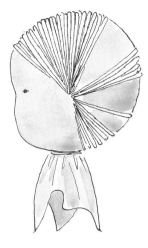

## The hair

The hair is stitched with knitting yarn. For a ponytail or shaggy style, center the stitches around the crown; for braids find a point just below each ear. With long straight stitches from the central point to the hairline, divide the hair into sections. For braids, mark a line lightly with pencil for the center part and take long stitches from each ear to the part and back. Not all stitches must be the full length, as they would then become too thick. Each section is then filled with long straight stitches very close together. For most styles, the ends can be left to hang free. Finally, several stitches are made either through individual strands of yarn or between them so that the hair is thick and the head is completely covered. For a ponytail, cut lengths of yarn, stitch each through the fabric once at the hairline, draw toward the back of the head, gathering up stray ends, and tie at the crown. Short, curly styles can be made by alternating loop stitches with short

tight stitches to lock the loops in place. For a shaggy style, the loops are longer and can be cut after lockstitching.

## The body

The body is made of flesh-colored woolen or cotton knit fabric (cotton jersey) or from an old thin knitted sweater.

1) Cut out according to the pattern, using the measurements only as a guideline according to the stretchiness of the knit fabric. Cut the arms long enough to reach down to the legs.

2) Sew the arms on the wrong side as shown by the dotted line and turn inside out to right side.

3) Stuff arms lightly up to the shoulders with wool. Keep the center area empty so that the arms can move freely. At the center of the shoulder fold, cut a tiny hole for neck and push excess head fabric through. Turn the raw edges under and sew firmly to neck.

4) Sew the back seam of the body from the top of legs to the shoulder; then stitch the legs and feet as shown by the dotted line. Clip carefully between the seams of the legs. Turn inside out to right side.

5) Stuff the legs to top of thighs; then with another ball of stuffing, begin to stuff the body. This enables the legs to move freely. Body and legs should be stuffed more firmly than arms. Stuff with one hand while forming and molding with the other.

6) Make a hole in the middle of the body stuffing and push the protruding wool from the neck cylinder into it. Draw the body fabric up over the center of arm section to the neck. Sew firmly to neck and close shoulder seams.

7) Turn the fabric under at armhole (do not cut), and sew to arms. Run a gathering stitch at wrists and draw up slightly.

8) Bend feet forward and up at a right angle and sew them to the leg. With small stitches, draw up ankle slightly, then stitch through ankle from side to side, pulling slightly to shape. So that the doll does not lose its form when laundered, wrap it in a towel and hang it to dry as in a hammock. One can also wash the doll's face with a sponge and soapy lather.

Seam allowance

Shoulder width
c. 2¾" (7 cm)

Back seam

Fold

Fold

1½ × head height

1½ × head height

7" (18 cm)

¾" (2 cm)

Foot

Fold     Neck opening     Fold

Seam     Open     Seam

c. 10" (26 cm)

c.1¼" (3 cm)

# Flopsy doll

*Materials:* white and flesh-colored cotton knit fabric; wool yarn for hair; wool stuffing; wool fabric, jersey or other soft, solid-colored fabric.

*Method:* The head is made as for the Formed Doll (page 58). The body is cut relatively large and is only lightly stuffed.

1) Cut out arms and body according to the diagram. Maximum stretch should run from wrist to wrist and across legs horizontally.

2) On leg section, on wrong side, sew back seam, then leg seams. Fold legs as though for pressing a crease in pants, then sew foot seam in a gentle curve from front to back. Turn inside out to right side.

3) Sew sleeve seams. Turn inside out to right side.

4) Cut a small hole at center of fold on arm section, pull surplus head fabric through the hole, turn under edge of neck hole and sew firmly to neck.

5) Form an oval-shaped bag from the surplus head fabric. Stuff with a handful of wool shaped into a solid oval cushion one and a half times the head height or 4" (10 cm). So that the head does not wobble, pull bottom edge of head covering down and sew to body cushion.

6) Stuff legs and lower body lightly, and

run a gathering thread through the upper edge.

7) Push body cushion down into lower section. Draw up thread and stitch raw edge firmly to cushion.

8) Pull upper section down, turn under raw edge and sew to lower section over gathering thread.

9) Cut out hands from flesh-colored knit, sew on wrong side as shown by dotted line. Turn through to right side and stuff lightly. Stuff arms lightly, draw up wrists, insert hands and sew in place.

10) Run a gathering thread around ankles and draw up slightly to indicate feet.

Gathering thread

Back seam

3" (7.5 cm)

Cutting seam

Fold

5¼" (13.5 cm)

← 2¾" (7 cm) → ← 2¾" (7 cm) →

← 5½" (14 cm) →

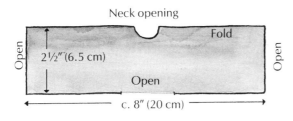

Neck opening

Fold

Open

2½" (6.5 cm)

Open

Open

← c. 8" (20 cm) →

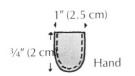

1" (2.5 cm)

¾" (2 cm)

Hand

# Doll's cloths and shawls

Many simple clothes from a baby's shawl to a grandmother's scarf can be made from solid-colored cloths. They should not be too harshly colored. To fix the cloths on the doll's head crown headbands (see page 31) can be made to a suitable size. Hem the edges.

*Materials:* Batiste, silk, thin woolen cloth, thin linen or flannel.

*Measurements:* 12" to 17" (30 to 50 cm) square.

# Doll's clothes

Five and six-year-old children already begin to sew clothes for their dolls. Usually the wish arises from observing an adult or older sibling who sews. It is especially good when a mother sews a doll's dress and perhaps even decorates it with embroidery, for this means that she is involved with this activity for quite a while and nonetheless is able to have time for her child as she works. As she works, she can also cut out fabric for the child to sew a doll's dress, and with tiny basting stitches can begin the first seam. The child will observe the mother's activity more and more closely, how she uses

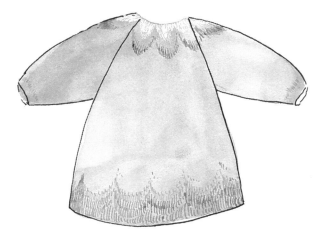

a thimble, how she threads the needle, how she sews a seam or sews on buttons, and will then want to do it just like the mother does.

The pattern for a doll's dress can be very simple. Thin, solid-colored wool fabric or other soft, solid-colored cotton fabrics such as flannel and batiste are appropriate fabrics for dolls' clothes.

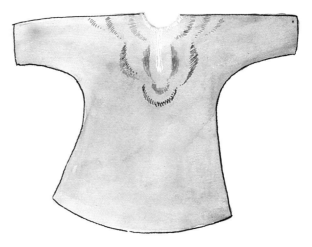

# Doll's bunting bed

Doll children, often wrapped in many cloths, find a secure protection in this bunting bed, in which they can be carried around. This makes for a cozy bundle for the child to snuggle in his or her arms. The bunting bed can also be laid in a basket or into a hanging hammock, or the child can lay it across the lap while listening to a story. At first, an adult or older child may be asked to tie the ribbons. Between age five and six, the normally developing child becomes interested in the tying process and then usually learns very quickly to tie through imitation.

This little bunting bed is a kind of thin mattress partly folded over to make a kind of sleeping bag. The head-end remains open and the top acts as a kind of blanket. The mattress is enclosed in a cover which can be removed for washing. The child "swaddles" its doll in this thinly stuffed mattress.

*Materials:* Batiste, poplin, muslin or flannel; unspun sheep's wool for stuffing.

*Measurements:* The finished bunting bed is 24" × 8½" (61 × 22 cm) big. The mattress material is 49" × 9" (124 × 23 cm). The cover material is 50" × 9½" (127 × 24 cm). The ties are ½" ribbon 24" long (1.5 × 60 cm).

*Method:*

1) Make the *mattress* first. Cut out the chosen material. Fold in half, pin together and seam around leaving the end open.
2) Turn right side out and stuff loosely with teased unspun wool (see page 52).
3) Close the end with small overhand stitches.
4) To prevent the wool from collecting in one corner, spread the stuffing evenly and fasten it with a few stitches.
5) Now make the *cover.* Cut out the material. Fold in half and place the ribbons in position.
6) Sew the two long sides with the ribbons firmly in the seam.
7) Turn right side out, put mattress inside.
8) Close the remaining seam with small overhand stitches.

When the child wants to tuck in its doll, it is put on the rounded pillow end, the little bunting bed is folded over and the ribbon, tied around, will keep dolly and bed in place.

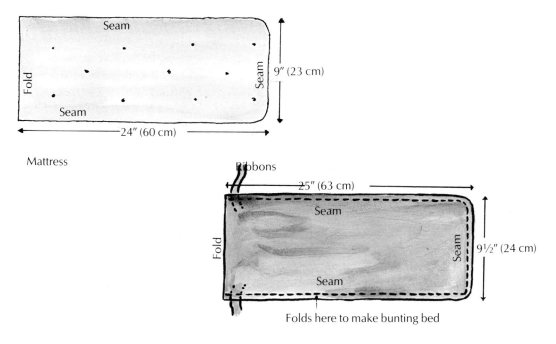

Mattress

Folds here to make bunting bed

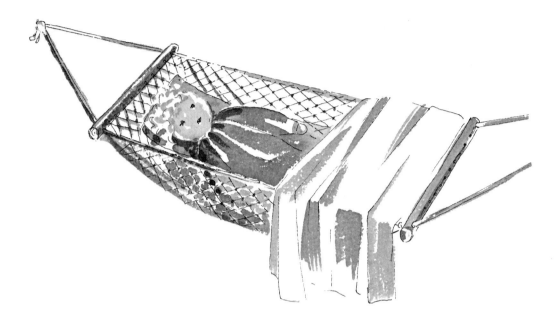

# Doll's hammock

*Materials:* A ball of thin string (60 yds, 50 m), 2 strips of plywood 8″ × ¾″ (20 × 2 cm), 2 pieces of dowel about 16″ (40 cm) long, 4 yds of thick string.

*Method:*
1) Suspend one of the strips of plywood at a convenient height for working.
2) Cut 40 lengths of string, each 50″ (125 cm) long.
3) Knot the strings together in pairs, leaving 4″ (10 cm) ends about the knots. Hang each pair astride the wood strip so that one length of string hangs behind the strip and one in front. Beginning at the left, strings are taken alternately from front and back and square-knotted together, thus: from first pair take the front string, from second pair the back one, knot them together; from second pair take the front string, from third pair the back one, and knot them. Continue to end of row. The first and last string of each row is missed, but will be knotted in the following row. Insert second plywood strip and continue knotting in similar fashion, but beginning with first string this time.

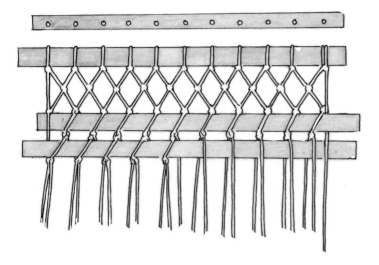

4) When the second row is completed, remove the first wood strip, and replace it with a length of string, which is then used to suspend the work.

5) Work 25 rows in all, again leaving about 4″ (10 cm) unused at ends of strings.

6) Bore twelve equally spaced holes in each dowel. Ignoring the end holes, draw four strings through each hole and make a large knot in each group to prevent them from slipping out again. (At the ends of the rows, there will be five or three strings per hole.)

7) The outside holes take the thick string by which the hammock will be sus-pended. This string is also threaded through the outside meshes and pulled somewhat taut, so that the hammock hangs well and the doll-babies do not fall out.

8) The thick string is use for hanging up the hammock. It is pulled through the end holes and threaded through the side net. Pull it a little shorter than the net to let the hammock sag in the middle and to prevent the dolls from falling out.

A hammock can also be crocheted like a ball net, using fine string. Other knotting and knotting techniques could also be used.

# The Play Store

In the age of the supermarket, a very simply equipped store corner can be of great significance for the child's play. Children still occasionally experience shops in which one must perhaps wait to be waited upon, where a customer is asked just what he is interested in buying, where a clerk brings out various items from which the customer may make a selection, and where one still hears "please" and "thank-you" and "you are welcome" on occasion. Such a play store allows children to imitate such social forms and interactions.

The play store consists of a playstand (page 25), perhaps with a roof covered by a play-cloth (page 29) fastened to the cross-pieces of the playstand and perhaps also attached to a molding on the wall, with a chair or stool and an additional shelf or playstand. The store is stocked with a wide variety of nicely cleaned nuts and fruit pits such as peaches, plums or apricots, with acorns and chestnuts neatly sorted into little baskets. Wooden scoops and small wooden bowls and baskets can be used for filling.

In this play store, the basic gestures of give and take, of please and thank-you are involved. We have also created a play area which will grow along with the children in their different developmental phases (see "Stages of Play", page 13) up to the seventh year and beyond, offering many oppoertunities for creative play. For the child under four the most important thing is the scooping and filling; for the four- and five-year-olds it is that there are enough "apples," "potatoes," and "eggs" in store. For the oldest children the exchange of money for purchases takes on increasing significance, along with the occasional construction of a "cash register" or a weighing scale. Older children also love to transform the whole store and its contents into a steamship, a tour bus, or an airplane.

Such fascinating things as real play money, a cash register, scales and real candies generally do not have the same inspiring effect on the creative play of the children.

# Carved wooden scoops, spoons and bowls

## Spoons and scoops

Those with a little experience in working with wood will find great pleasure in carving these simple objects. They each then become unique and provide the children with a variety of living impressions as they use them.

*Materials:* Wood: birch, maple, mahogany basswood, or perhaps scraps from a cabinet maker.

*Tools:* workbench with vice, if possible; whittling knife, gouge, saw, rasp or file, sand paper.

*Method:*

1) With a pencil, mark the form of the spoon on the top of the wood block as shown in diagram. Make sure that the grain runs along the length of the spoon or scoop.

2) Cut away the wood outside the outlined form with a fine saw or whittling knife, so that a smooth surface is created all around.

3) Draw the curved view of the spoon or scoop on the side surface of the block; again cut away the wood outside the outline, making sure that the surface is smooth.

4) Round off the edges with a rasp so that the form is pleasant to hold.

5) Draw the outline of the form to be carved out (see dotted line in diagram) making sure to leave a thick enough edge.

6) Carefully gouge out the depression, always carving towards the center. Keep looking at and feeling the wood from all sides until the form has finally been achieved.

7) Finally, sand the surface smooth with sandpaper, rub with beeswax (see Resource List), and buff to a shine.

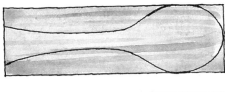

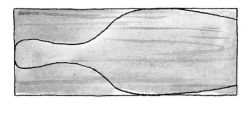

# Bowls

*Method:*

1) Draw the desired form onto the block of wood.

2) Leaving a sufficiently thick edge all the way around, slowly hollow out the center of the bowl with the gouge, following the grain.

3) After hollowing out the center, cut away the wood outside the outline with a whittling knife or fine saw.

4) Draw the size of the base of the bowl on the bottom of the block. Cut away the excess wood around this base, creating a rounded form.

5) Finish off the upper edge with the whittling knife in such a way that the outer edge is slightly lower than the inner edge, for example, so that the top surface of the edge slopes slightly toward the outside.

6) Sand all surfaces smooth with sand paper, rub with beeswax, and polish or buff to a shine.

# Dollhouse

Playing with a dollhouse is especially loved by six- to nine-year-olds. Children's attention spans are then long enough that they can spend a long time completely engrossed in such play, forgetting all that is happening around them. Play now consists of building; rearranging; remodelling; adding on new rooms or a garden, a barn or a meadow; making new dolls or dolls' clothes; sewing or knitting rugs; sewing pillows and blankets for the beds; building little shelves from log slices and little boards and filling them with dishes (acorn caps or tiny shells). Most of all, children love to spread all this out around them on a large table or on the floor.

It is important to support the children's joy of discovery and invention by supplying only the raw materials. One should consciously avoid indulging one's justifiable adult delight in perfect miniature objects.

*Materials:* 16" × 20" (40 × 50 cm) wooden board; 3 pieces of basket cane or willow 37", 35" and 33" (95, 90, 85 cm) long and ⁵⁄₁₆" (8 mm) thick; a piece of thin cotton fabric, such as batiste, 31" × 39" (80 × 100 cm).

*Method:*
1) Cut off corners of wood to achieve a pleasant, rounded shape.
2) Drill six holes the diameter of the cane, as shown in diagram.
3) Sand and wax the wood.
4) Insert cane in holes to form three arches, the shortest piece at the back, the longest at the front.
5) Iron fabric well and attach one side to front arch with a few stitches. At the back, draw the fabric together with a gathering thread. The fabric can also simply be draped over the three cane arches and the children can fasten it with clothespins, knots or woolen cords.

Building logs (page 37), especially branch pieces or long, thin branches or branches split lengthwise, and small building cloths (page 37) and yarn cords (page 32) enhance and complete the play possibilities with the little dollhouse.

c. 31″ x 39″ (80 x 100 cm)

Cotton fabric

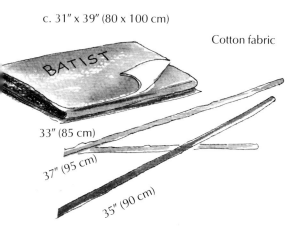

BATIST

33″ (85 cm)

37″ (95 cm)

35″ (90 cm)

wooden board

c. 16″ x 20″ (40 x 50 cm)

# Carved wooden furniture for the dollhouse

*Materials:* Wooden branches (birch, maple, chestnut, and so on); saw, whittling knife or pocket knife, gouge; beeswax balsam for finished surfaces.

## Chair

Cut through a branch 6"–7" (16–18 cm) long, 3" (7–8 cm) diameter at an angle of 45° in order to create wooden pieces for two chairs. With a gouge, carve out the seat surface. Round off the edges with a knife.

## Table

Cut off a branch about 3" (7 cm) long, 3" in diameter. Carve out the base in the direction indicated by arrows in the diagram. One can also simply place a larger wooden slice on top of a smaller one.

## Beds

Cut a round branch about 5" (12 cm) long and 3" (8 cm) diameter lengthwise with a saw or a hatchet. Carve out the inner surface with a gouge and round off the edges with a knife. The base can be flattened a little with the knife. These pieces can also be used as boats or as a roof when placed onto two shorter pieces.

# Dolls for the dollhouse

The small dolls can be knotted from a piece of thin fabric and dressed in a simple dress or apron (see knotted dolls, page 54). One can also take standing dolls (page 45) and make arms for them.

*Method:*

1) Cut lightweight fabric for arms in proportion to the doll's size.

2) Sew arms as shown in diagram.

3) Pull the fabric ends from the head through the neck hole and then stitch all around the neck.

4) Cut in the felt a bit at both shoulders to make armholes. Set in the sleeve piece and sew the felt onto the head. Fill the arms with a bit of sheep's wool. Gather at the wrists and sew on small hands (see directions for Flopsy Doll, page 62).

Men can be given a hat so that they are appropriately characterized.

School-age children also like to knit dolls for themselves. They will need help with proportions, increasing and decreasing, and stitching the pieces together (see knitted dolls, page 78). Children who prefer to sew may make dolls such as standing dolls or simple unformed dolls. Or they may shape the doll out of pipe cleaners and wrap the figure with unspun sheep's wool.

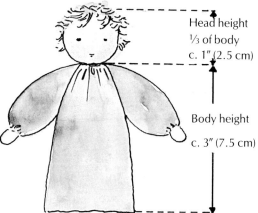

Head height
⅓ of body
c. 1" (2.5 cm)

Body height

c. 3" (7.5 cm)

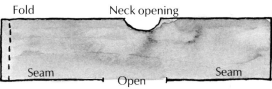

Fold

Neck opening

Seam

Seam

Open

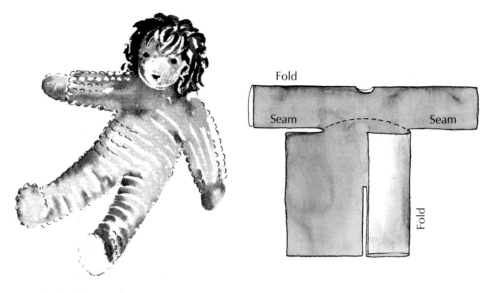

# Knitted doll

*Materials:* One pair knitting needles (size 5 or 6, 4 or 4.5 mm), 1 oz (25 g) wool yarn (worsted weight, double knitting), wool stuffing, yarn for hair, cotton knit (cotton jersey) fabric for head.

*Method:* Knit every row.
1) Cast on 40 stitches, and knit 14 rows.
2) Next row, knit 19, knit 2 stitches together, loop yarn over needle to make a little hole for the neck. Knit to end of row.
3) Knit 14 rows (40 stitches).
4) Bind off 13 stitches, knit to end of row.
5) Bind off 13 stitches, knit to end of row, cast on 7 stitches.
6) Knit to end of row, cast on 7 stitches.
7) Knit 16 rows.
8) Knit 14 stitches, put other 14 stitches on a holder.
9) Knit back and forth on 14 stitches for 34 rows; bind off, leaving 24" (60 cm) length of yarn.
10) Put stitches from holder on needle and repeat knitting back and forth on 14 stitches for 34 rows; bind off, again leaving 24" (60 cm) length of yarn.

*To Make Up:* Using the loose end of yarn, sew, weave, or crochet doll together as follows:
1) Fold each leg lengthwise; sew up each leg seam.
2) Fold over upper body and sew sleeves toward center.

If you sew neatly, you do not need to turn inside out; otherwise, turn inside out.

Make hands and head as for formed doll (page 61 and 58). (In proportion with this body, the head should be about

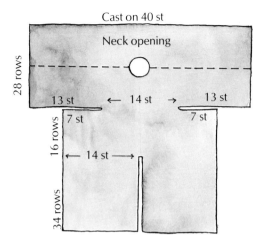

Cast on 40 st

Neck opening

28 rows

13 st ← 14 st → 13 st

16 rows 7 st 7 st

34 rows ← 14 st →

2", 5 cm high.) Draw up sleeve ends to fit wrists, and sew hands in place. Push surplus fabric of head through neck hole into body, and stitch head to body firmly at neck. Stuff arms, legs and body lightly and sew center back.

# Simple String Puppets or Marionettes

Five or six-year-olds who see marionette plays performed by adults or older siblings often are stimulated to imitate such plays. In the absence of simple string puppets or marionettes, children will take a knot doll and tie strings around the neck so that the doll can be moved as the story is told. Here are instructions for very simple, sturdy marionettes for daily use rather than for special occasions

*Materials:* Simple, solid-colored fabric remnants; wool or cotton thread; unspun sheep's wool: white for stuffing and yellow, brown, or gray for hair.

The characters are indicated by the color of their garments (capes, veils, cloaks, and so on). For example, a golden cloak and golden crown for a *king.*
*Queen:* light blue or rose gown with blue cloak and golden crown.
*Prince:* golden yellow gown with gold or red cape or cloak.
*Princess:* pink gown with pale pink or white cloak.
*Old Man:* blue-violet garment.
*Old Woman:* red-violet garment with veil.

With subtle colors, the entire figure can be dressed in one piece of fabric.

Cloaks, capes or veils are added in stronger or different colors. The size measurements can, of course, be varied as desired.

*Method:*

1) Roll well-fluffed sheep's wool into a cylinder about 5" (12 cm) long. Tie off about 2" (5 cm) for the head (see page 80).

2) Cover the round head with a square of fabric (about 16" (40 cm) square) and tie off at the neck, making sure that ends hang
equally.

3) Take two opposite ends for the arms. Turn the ends under so that arms are about 4" (11 cm) long; tie off at wrists.

4) Round off the other two corners for the gown so that it is about 7" (17 cm) long (see diagram).

5) Wrap the wool cylinder lightly. It allows the figure to sit without collapsing. If the figure is to stand up, the cylinder must be 6" (15 cm) long below the neckline (see diagram page 80).

6) Sew on loosely arranged colored sheep's wool for hair.

7) Add cloak, veil or cape, and crown or kerchief as desired.

8) The head can be covered with a pale pink fabric and the
garment can be sewn of another fabric, as indicated in the accompanying diagram. Cut out sleeves and garments and sew seams as shown.

9) Fasten the sleeves at the neckline. Gather sleeves at wrist and sew on hands made by covering oval-shaped sheep's wool with bits of fabric from the face fabric.

10) Close the back seam and shoulder seams. Cut in 1½" (4 cm) for the armholes on each side. Run a gathering stitch around the neck hole, draw it tight

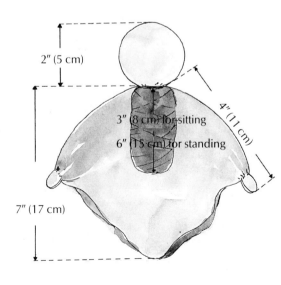

2" (5 cm)

3" (8 cm) for sitting
6" (15 cm) for standing

4" (11 cm)

7" (17 cm)

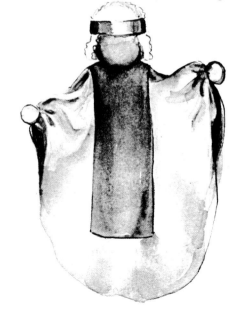

and stitch around the neckline. With some fabric it may be desireable to run a second gathering stitch about 1½″ (4 cm) below the neckline and lightly pull it to create a more flowing garment (see diagram at far right).

For strings, twist a simple wool yarn strand or embroidery floss in the color of the garment into a thin cord. Attach it to the side of the head at the ears, making the end of the cord as invisible as possible. The cord should reach 10″ (25 cm) above the head of the marionette.

Garment

Seam

5/8″ (1.5 cm)

Cut 1½″ (4 cm)

6¾″ (17 cm)

Fold

Seam at back

Fold

c. 6″ (15 cm)

Sleeves

Fold    Neck hole    Fold

2¼″ (6 cm)

8¾″ (22 cm)

Seam    Seam

3¼″ (8 cm)    Open

10″ (25 cm)

8″ (20 cm)

## The stage

Create a landscape on the floor, on a broad bench or a low table, using building logs surrounded by colored cloths. As an adult or child narrates the story, the marionettes are gently guided through the landscape (without hopping up and down).

# Knitted Animals

Knitted animals such as the ones described here are intended for children of five years and older. Only then, when the powers of imagination awaken more fully, can the child use such toys meaningfully in creative play, building stables, leading them out to pasture, and providing "feed" and "water." It is good to keep such animals small enough so that they can be used appropriately in creative play landscapes. If children have never had the opportunity to experience the life of animals, on a farm for example, then they will also be unlikely to be stimulated to play with such toy animals. Through tabletop puppet plays, through verses and stories, however, one can provide children with sufficient stimulation for their play. One should also see to it that children do not have too many animals; during the developmental phase of imitation, doll play is always the most appropriate and meaningful.

## Sheep

*Materials:* Natural, undyed knitting yarn; unspun sheep's wool; two knitting needles.

*Knitting technique:* Garter stitch (knit each stitch across every row).

*Method:* Knit the body of the sheep according to the diagram. In the instructions the first figure is for a large sheep, the second for a medium-sized sheep, and the last figure is for a very tiny lamb.

*To form the sheep:*
1) Fold the head at "O" and sew bound-off edges together on wrong side of work.
2) With a few gathering stitches, bring "X" to "A" at each side, pulling slightly as

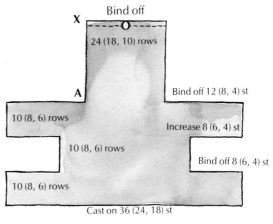

Bind off

X — O —
24 (18, 10) rows

A                Bind off 12 (8, 4) st

10 (8, 6) rows

Increase 8 (6, 4) st

10 (8, 6) rows

Bind off 8 (6, 4) st

10 (8, 6) rows

Cast on 36 (24, 18) st

Begin here

you stitch. Shape the resulting ears with a few stitches.

3) Sew wrong sides of leg seams and stomach seam together, leaving the rear opening free for stuffing.

4) Turn to right side, stuff legs, using a long strand for each leg that reaches into the stomach cavity and thus prevents the legs from folding. (Wrapping the wool tightly around the point of scissors works well for this.)

5) Stuff the body of the sheep, not quite as firmly as the legs. Shape with one hand while you stuff with the other.

6) Sew up remaining seam.

7) Add a tail of crocheted yarn or a twisted cord of wool.

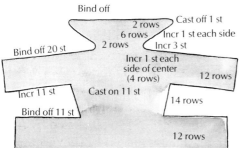

Bind off

2 rows      Cast off 1 st

6 rows      Incr 1 st each side

Bind off 20 st     2 rows     Incr 3 st

Incr 1 st each side of center (4 rows)     12 rows

Incr 11 st     Cast on 11 st

Bind off 11 st     14 rows

12 rows

Cast on 40 st

Begin here

# Horse

*Material:* approximately 1 oz (20 g) of knitting yarn for the body; about 2 yards of wool yarn for the mane and tail; about 1 oz (20 g) of unspun wool for stuffing; two knitting needles.

*Knitting technique:* Garter stitch (knit each stitch across every row).

*Method:* Begin with the *body*

1) Cast on 40 stitches and knit 12 rows.

2) Bind off 11 stitches at the beginning of each of next 2 rows.

3) Knit 14 rows

4) Cast on 11 stitches on each of the next 2 rows.

5) In the middle of the next row, after the twentieth stitch, increase 11 stitches all at once. This will make it easier to shape the horse later on.

6) Knit one row. Then in every second

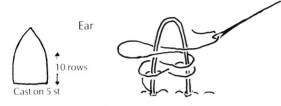

Ear

10 rows

Cast on 5 st

row, increase 1 stitch before and after the middle stitch in the row. Continue for 12 rows.

7) Bind off 20 stitches at the beginning of each of the next two rows.

8) With the remaining 19 stitches, knit 2 rows.

9) Now increase 3 stitches at the beginning of each of the next two rows.

10) Then increase 1 stitch on each side for each of the next two rows on each side.

11) After the 6 rows for the head, decrease one stitch on each side in the next row.

12) Bind off.

13) To make the *ears* cast on 5 stitches.

14) Knit 10 rows knitting together the second and third stitch in each row. The ears can also be formed by using a woolen loop directly on the head. Simply weave the yarn through the loop from bottom to top, pulling slightly together so that the ear becomes pointed (see diagram).

## Forming the horse

1) After binding off, sew closed the hole in the back, then sew seams at head, legs and stomach, closing the seams from the outside. Leave the rear opening free for stuffing.

2) Stuff the head and neck firmly, but not too tightly. For the legs, wind the wool around scissors until one can no longer rotate the scissors inside the wool. Then pull out the scissors and stuff this stiff strand into the legs, using one strand for each leg. The strand should extend deep into the body to help support the legs when the horse stands. Finally, stuff the stomach firmly, because this is where the child will hold the horse. Stuffing demands a certain feeling and finesse in forming, especially with the left hand. Make sure that the legs are all the same length and all reach the ground.

3) Close the rear opening up to the hole for the tail.

4) Sew the ears on in the appropriate places by holding together the lower corners so that a rounded ear is created.

5) To make the *mane* stitch along the entire neck up to the forehead. Take a stitch, leave end free, then insert the needle again into the same stitch. Pull through and cut in desired length (see diagram A). Repeat all along the neck.

6) Continue the same stitches now in the other direction, 2 or 3 rows side by side. In this way, the mane will stand up. (See diagram B.)

7) To make the *tail* wrap the wool around your hand. Stitch the loop to the horse. Cut open loops at the end.

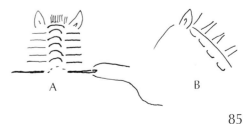

A

B

# Hens and roosters

*Material:* Knitting yarn, white or yellow for the body, red for the comb; unspun wool for stuffing; 2 knitting needles

*Knitting technique:* Garter stitch (knit each stitch across every row).

*Method:*
1) Cast on for example 16 stitches (the size can be increased or decreased).
2) Knit a square and then bind off.
3) Fold in half diagonally.
4) Sew one side closed. Fill with sheep's wool; sew second side closed.
5) From the bottom point, take one gathering stitch to the center of the top and then back again to the lower point to form the typical hen shape.
6) The comb atop the head can be made with a few buttonhole stitches at the neck with red yarn.

# Pigs

*Materials:* Pink wool yarn; unspun sheep's wool; 2 knitting needles.

*Knitting technique:* Garter stitch (knit each stitch across every row).

*Method:* Begin with the body.
1) Cast on 36 stitches. Knit 12 rows.
2) Bind off 5 stitches at the beginning of each of the two next rows.
3) Knit 12 rows.
4) Cast on 5 stitches at the beginning of each of the next 2 rows.
5) Knit 12 rows.
6) Bind off 7 stitches at the beginning of each of the next 2 rows, knitting only 4 rows.
7) In each of the next 6 rows, decrease one stitch both to the right and to the left of the center stitch.
8) Knit one row without decreasing.
9) In the next row, again decrease one stitch to the left and to the right of the center two stitches.
10) Repeat steps 8 and 9.
11) Bind off the remaining 6 stitches.
12) To make the *ears* cast on 5 stitches.
13) Knit 9 rows.
14) In each of the remaining rows to the end, knit together the second and third stitches.
15) To *complete* sew together the head, stomach and leg seams. Leave an opening at the rear for stuffing.
16) Stuff the head and body with wool and close the rear seam.

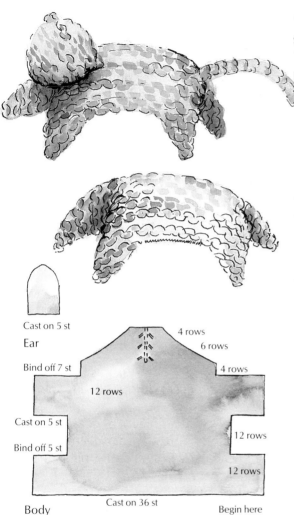

17) A curly tail from twisted wool can be sewn on.

18) Sew on the ears at the appropriate places.

# Cat

*Materials:* Wool knitting yarn (silver gray, white or beige); 2 knitting needles; unspun sheep's wool for stuffing.

*Knitting technique:* Garter stitch (knit each stitch across every row).

*Method:*

1) Cast on 16 stitches.

2) Knit a rectangle which is slightly shorter than a square (about 24 rows).

3) Cast off remaining stitches.

4) Sew the corners like cones, so that the legs are formed.

5) Stuff the body and close the stomach seam.

6) To make the *head* cast on 7 stitches.

7) Knit about 20 rows. The piece should be twice as long as its width.

8) Fold in half. Stuff with wool and close seams.

9) Pull in the lower seam so that the head is nice and round.

10) With a few stitches, form little ears.

11) Sew the head onto the body.

12) To make the *tail* cast on 3 stitches.

13) Knit about 20 rows.

14) Sew together lengthwise and then attach to body.

Cast on 5 st

Ear

Bind off 7 st

4 rows

6 rows

4 rows

12 rows

Cast on 5 st

Bind off 5 st

12 rows

12 rows

Body

Cast on 36 st

Begin here

# Donkey

*Materials:* Grey knitting yarn, dark grey yarn for the mane; unspun wool for stuffing; 2 knitting needles, size 6 (4.5 mm).

*Knitting technique:* Garter stitch (knit each stitch across every row).

*Method:* Begin with the body.
1) Cast on 40 stitches, and knit 12 rows.
2) Cast off 11 stitches at the beginning of each of the next two rows.
3) Knit 14 rows.
4) Increase 11 stitches at the beginning of each of the next two rows. To the right and to the left of the two middle stitches, increase one stitch in every second row (7 times, until 54 stitches are on the needle).
5) Bind off 16 stitches at the beginning of each of the next two rows.
6) In the next row, increase one stitch on the right and one stitch on the left of the middle stitch in the row.
7) At the beginning of each of the next two rows, decrease 2 stitches.
8) At the beginning of each of the next two rows, knit two stitches together.
9) Increase 3 stitches at the beginning of each of the next two rows.
10) Increase 2 stitches at the beginning of each of the next two rows.
11) Knit 4 rows.
12) At the beginning of the next two rows, knit together two stitches each time.

13) Cast off remaining stitches.
14) To make the ears cast on 5 stitches.
15) Knit 14 rows.
16) In each successive row, knit together the second and third stitch.
17) Sew seams together and stuff (see directions for horse, page 84).
18) With dark yarn, sew on the mane as described for the horse. 19) For the tail, attach three strands of yarn. Wrap them and add a tassel of dark yarn at the tip of the tail.

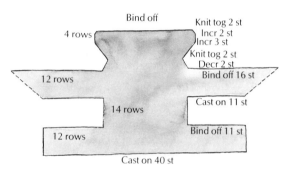

# Ducks

*Materials:* Lightweight knitting yarn; un-spun wool for stuffing; 2 knitting needles

*Knitting technique:* Garter stitch (knit each stitch across every row).

*Method:* Begin with the body
1) Cast on 30 stitches.
2) Knit 20 rows, then cast off.
3) Fold in half lengthwise.
4) Close the lower seam and rear seam, making sure that lower edges are rounded off.
5) Stuff with sheep's wool and close the upper seam. Form with one hand as you stuff with the other.

6) For the *head* cast on 16 stitches.
7) Knit 12 rows, then cast off.
8) Fold in half lengthwise. Sew two seams closed.
9) Stuff with wool; then close the third seam. Make sure that the head is oval shaped.
10) Sew the head to the body.
11) For the *beak* sew on two loops at the front of the head. Weave in and out of the loops with the sewing needle (see directions for horse's ear, page 84) until the loops are completely filled.
12) For the *eyes* sew on eyes with 2 to 3 stitches.

# Tumbling Man

For special occasions, for example when a child is ill or must be kept waiting, this little tumbling man can provide a welcome distraction. A simple wooden board, a small table or an ironing board tilted at an angle can serve as a tumbling surface. If the surface is too smooth, it can be covered with a play-cloth or a woolen blanket.

*Materials:* Felt pieces; glass marble or round weight ¾" to 1" (2 to 2.5 cm) diameter; cardboard tube 1¼" (3 cm) diameter made from kitchen or toilet tissue roll; small scraps of fabric; glue.

*Method:*

1) Cut out the suit or dress of the tumbling man (cut out double) as in illustration. Hands and feet can be cut out of the same piece or cut out separately from beige felt.

2) Sew the two large fabric pieces together with a running stitch (not a buttonhole stitch). Choose thread in the color of the felt. Include the hands and feet in the seam if needed.

3) Cut the cardboard tube to about half as long again as the diameter of the glass marble. For example, for a marble of 1" (25 mm) diameter, a cardboard tube of 1½" (4 cm) in length.

4) Place the marble in the cardboard tube and glue fabric over the opening at both ends, making sure not to overlap too far down the tube where the face will be.

5) Glue a narrow strip of beige felt or cotton knit over the tube as a face.

6) Glue head into neck opening of felt suit or dress.

7) Add hair or beard of sheep's wool as desired.

8) A cap can be sewn on, as long as it is

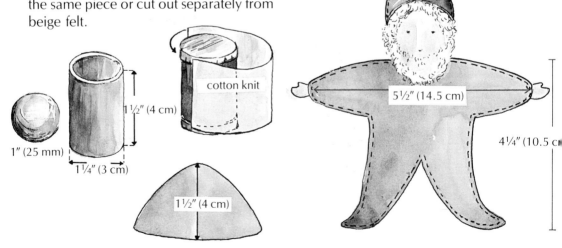

cotton knit

1½" (4 cm)

1" (25 mm)

1¼" (3 cm)

1½" (4 cm)

5½" (14.5 cm)

4¼" (10.5 cm)

not so large that it interferes with the somersaults.

9) Eyes and mouth can be lightly indicated with colored pencil.

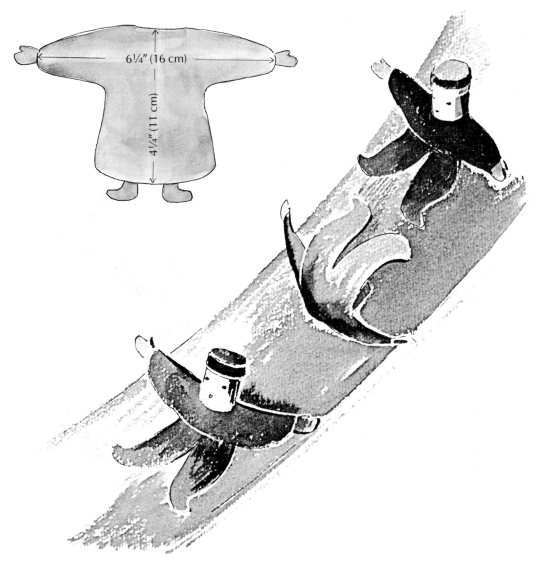

6¼" (16 cm)

4¼" (11 cm)

# Making Pictures with Plant-Dyed Wool

For older children, five and six-year-olds, one can hang a blue or natural white woolen, felt or melton cloth on the wall, on which the children can create colored wool pictures. The fluffs of wool must be especially delicate and thin and can then be simply pressed in place on the cloth. At first, children will need the help of an adult who is able to spend time patiently with them in creating such pictures.

It is preferable to work with surfaces of color rather than with outlined forms, such as that of a house, for example. The children will imitate this approach. This activity is particularly suited for wintertime.

# Recommended Reading

Willi Aeppli, *Care and Development of the Human Senses,* Steiner Press, London.

Heidi Britz-Crecelius, *Children At Play: Preparation for Life,* Floris Books, Edinburgh, and Inner Traditions, Vermont.

Elisabeth Grunelius, *Early Childhood Education and the Waldorf School Plan,* Waldorf Monographs, Garden City, New York.

A. C. Harwood, *The Way of a Child,* Rudolf Steiner Press, London.

Rudolf Steiner, *The Education of the Child in the Light of Anthroposophy,* Steiner Press, London, and Anthroposophic Press, New York.

Caroline von Heydebrand, *Childhood: A Study of the Growing Soul,* Steiner Press, London.

Wilhelm zur Linden, *When a Child is Born,* Thorsons, New York, and *A Child is Born,* Steiner Press, London.

# Resource List

## Sheep's wool and stuffing

Wilde Yarns
3705 Main Street
Philadelphia, PA 19127

West Earl Woolen Mill
Ephrata, PA 17522

Bartlett Yarns
P.O. Box 36
Harmony, ME 04942
(207) 683-2251

## Silk

Sureway Trading Enterprises
826 Pine Avenue, Suite 5 & 6
Niagara Falls, NY 14301

Thai Silks
252 State Street
Los Altos, CA 94022

## Plant-dyed wool, wool felt, and cotton knit

Child's Play
161 Naples Road
Brookline, MA 02146
(617) 734-2605

## Beeswax paste and other organic wood finishes

Woodpecker's Tools, Inc.
614 Agua Fria Street
Santa Fe, NM 87501
(505) 988-2288

## Natural dyes

Alliance Import Company
1021 "R" Street One
Sacramento, CA 95814
(916) 920-8658 (800) 327-8448

Earth Guild
Tingle Alley
Asheville, NC 28801

## Children's harps

Choroi Musical Instruments
Karen Klaveness
4600 Minnesota Avenue
Fair Oaks, CA 95628
(916) 966-1227

## Toys and children's art supplies

The Ark
4245 Crestline Avenue
Fair Oaks, CA 95628
(916) 593-0712

Heartwood Arts
RD 1, Box 126, Rtes. 44/45
Modena, NY 12548
(914) 883-5145

Hearth Song
P.O. Box B
Sebastopol, CA 95473
(707) 829-1550

Hans Schumm Woodworks
RD 2, Box 233
Ghent, NY 12075
(518) 672-4685

Check your local classified directory for stores specializing in fabric, weaving, knitting, and quilting supplies.